*note* [handwritten]

# For the Sake of America

*Feb 1st/21* [handwritten]

[handwritten note:] When I first heard of Shiela on "His Glory" network with Dave & Amanda I decided to buy all (5) of her books on "FOR THE SAKE OF AMERICA" then 3 more of hers so lots of Info Straight Insights from God as she's a Prophetess as well!

## America is in Trouble

### The Root Problems and the
### Promises of the LORD are Revealed
### For The Sake Of America!

Sheila Holm

### Three Weeks In Georgia Turned Into

*'Assignment Georgia: For The Sake Of America'*

*For the Sake of America*

# *For the Sake of America*

ISBN-10: 537541749

ISBN-13: 978-1537541747

Unless otherwise indicated all scriptures are taken from the
New King James version of the Bible.

http://hisbest4us.org

Facebook: HISBest4us and Sheila Holm Christian Author

Printed in USA by HIS Best Publishing

# DEDICATION

To Tommy and Penelope Wilson for praying while sitting behind me at Blackville Church of God and for saying, *What God has revealed to you needs to be in a book. Believers need to know the truth.* Trusted another book was not 'in the plan' but, the LORD confirmed the word the same day, two weeks ago!

To Michael and Denita Turner for opening your home to host me when I was at the point of leaving Georgia, for arranging opportunities so I can share the truth with believers in the region, for providing peace and protection which is required during the days and nights of researching and typing this book, a book which would not be in print if I had left Georgia due to not seeing an open door to complete upon the assignment.

To Bill Morford for remaining obedient until the One New Man Bible Revealing Jewish Roots and Power was translated direct from Hebrew and made available to all Christians so believers will see and know the truth: *We are no longer Gentiles, and we are not to do as the Gentiles do!*

To Rebecca King for providing the truth about the glory for the truth is: *Christ gave us the glory before He went to the cross, so we would be one as He and the Father are one.* **John 17:22.**

To Rebecca Lambert for your willingness to be filled with faith while praying and editing, especially since the depth of what the LORD has revealed is beyond human comprehension.

To Kirk Cameron for all of the effort to produce and distribute the film *Monumental,* for providing the truth about the Pilgrims, the Faith Monument, how America became a blessed nation with liberty and freedom for all, and for the research by David Barton, so all believers in America will be reminded of the truth!

To the many who have strengthened me the past 25 years, to those who have challenged me, hosted me, helped to secure assets in California and Georgia while I am traveling: Paul, Debbie, Lisa and Frank. To Paula for donating the car in Georgia. To those who have walked in faith, believing while the LORD has taken me to each nation in preparation for Georgia after directing the specific items to pack within one suitcase plus the instruction to 'bring the lap top' for a three week trip to Macon, Georgia. To my family and friends for praying through and standing firm with me during these unique days in HIStory!

To all citizens who are believers in the only one true living LORD who will stand firm in these days to take back what the enemy stole from our lives, States and America, especially to the Pilgrims who sacrificed all so the truth would be brought to America and become available to all who seek the word, the truth. To the mighty men and women of the LORD who persevered through all situations even becoming martyrs so the bible would be translated into English (Tyndale; DVD title, *God's Outlaw*).

To all Native Americans, especially the Creek who were the largest tribe north of Mexico until land was stolen due to invalid treaties.

*a great knowledgable (Historian)*

# Table of Contents

# Introduction

Our LORD has a tremendous sense of humor!

The LORD sent me to Kuala Lumpur, Malaysia during Ramadan. He knew I did not have any knowledge about the country or that it is a Muslim country which operates on their own calendar for their holidays.

Moments before my flight home, the LORD arranged an invitation for me to fly to Shanghai, China and due to the reception there I was invited to continue the journey to Shenzhen, China.

Years before, the LORD arranged a business trip to Japan. It was my first trip 'outside of America'. It was a very tough business trip to share with my Dad because he served in the Orient, from New Guinea, through the islands, to the Philippines during WWII as an Army Medic immediately after the bombing of Pearl Harbor.

9

The LORD has placed my feet on the soil of nearly all continents and all of the training in all of the nations prior to this day aligns with His purpose for these days.

Only He knew what it would require. Only He knew I would remain in Georgia until the truth is revealed. Some points were not revealed until I prepared this book. Only He knew America would head straight into a major crisis if the body of Christ was not awake, long before we realized 'as a people' that America is in deep trouble.

Now, as Americans, we have finally reached a tipping point. Therefore, the story can be told to all who will hear the truth! Why? More Christians are 'awake' and more is being revealed, even by the media, within days and hours than ever before in our history. The good news: The LORD has BIG plans for each of us! We merely need to 'walk it out in FAITH' as He directs.

So much of the 'what happened' was kept from the people in America. When a few were informed, they did not think it would be right to question the government. Individually we can do all Christ did while on earth and more! How do I know?

1. Christ said it while He was 'on earth'.

2. What He has done through me causes me to stand in awe!

3. What He has shown me regarding each of the roots which affect everything about our lives and our future in America today is beyond human comprehension so it is time for Christians to align in one accord and repair the breach!

After stating *Jesus take my hand and bring me through or take me home* more times than I can count, He took my hand when I was in a fetal position and I declared, *I am done, there is nothing else I can do.* In the very next moment I heard His quiet voice reminding me, *Through Me you can do all things.*

### If We Viewed Our Life Through God's Eyes
### If We Only Spoke His Truth

We often hear the question or we ask it, *Who's report do we believe?*

The LORD sent me to nearly every continent to realize the difference in how the people represent Him in other nations vs. how we speak about who He is in our lives in America.

**Example: Conversation with the driver assigned to me in London.** She was fascinated with Americans. She wanted to know details about my life in America. Without realizing it, I was 'speaking American' to her, a term which is used globally since we talk about our personal 'stuff' and the 'traumatic news of the day' regarding what 'we are dealing with' vs. what our LORD is doing in our life as a testimony to who He is in our life.

Within a few moments I was sliding in the seat while she swerved the car as she jerked the wheel and exited the M25 at high speed, slammed on the brakes, turned around and asked me a very simple question: *Do we serve the same God?*

Everything came to a complete halt.

The car was not moving.

Silence inside the vehicle even though cars were passing at high speed.

No words came forth from me.

Shocked. Stunned.

It was a deeper question she was asking in her stiff Nigerian and British mixed accent, especially since I was on the way to a conference where I was going to be representing the only living LORD.

A quick checklist was going through my mind: 1. I trust I truly do represent Him, 2. I trust I only serve Him.

My heart was heavy because she was not hearing anything from me about the LORD I serve, the LORD who has brought me out of the depths of a debacle no humans have been able to resolve.

That is the truth. However, I was only talking to her from my human perspective as an American. The 'American perspective' is what Christians 'find odd' as I travel nation to nation!

My driver had recently escaped from severe conditions in Nigeria.

She was grateful the LORD placed her in London. As she began to tell me a few of her testimonies from just the past few days, tears welled up in my eyes.

From birth, her only provider was the LORD. She did not have the options or resources in Nigeria for her to survive. Her family had nothing to offer her so she lived off the streets for as long as she could remember.

She came from nothing and the LORD has given her everything!

She has a beautiful car which the LORD provided and more than enough for her to take the day off to meet the woman of God from America. She was honored and yet, she was hearing nothing about the glorious life our LORD orchestrates for us day after day.

**America**. Being as blessed as we are in America, can we fast from our human understanding or from food? Can we fast from the news or from TV or from the internet for one day, or two?

Can we?

**Roots.** So many issues to address but, the LORD reminds me each day to only focus upon the roots. Roots need to be dealt with and repented for, and that is His focus for this book!

**More about London.** Later that evening, I was hosted by a couple from Nigeria. The wife was recovering from major surgery and just returned home moments before their pastor called.

When the pastor heard about her surgery, he cautioned her husband since he trusted they would not want to host someone from America during his wife's recovery. The pastor was surprised to hear the husband's response, ***Bring the woman of God to our home for we want to bless the woman of God so the LORD's blessings will come upon us, our home, and flood into our lives.***

Upon my arrival in the home, without having a conversation, my hostess experienced immediate healing. The LORD blessed me. He blessed my hosts, their lives and their home.

13

Her testimony was as deep as the one shared by my driver.

She escaped from Nigeria with only the shirt on her back.

She was homeless when she arrived. Now, she is the Director of the Housing Authority helping all who are homeless in the region. She gives all credit to God!

My host asked how the LORD operates through me. I told him the most simple answer as it came direct from the LORD when I opened my mouth, *All I have to do is show up.*

My host remembered this statement and used it during a special meeting in London which brought together people from many fellowships. A well known man from Holland was going to fly in to be the speaker.

When the leader of the gathering started the meeting, he introduced my host.

Without hesitation my host said, *The speaker missed his flight but, we have a speaker from America and she does not need any notice...*

Needless to say, I was immediately in a conversation with the LORD since I did not have prayer time with Him about this gathering. Immediate, private and silent prayers seeking the words the LORD wanted me to share with His people.

Months later, I was back in London and the pastor of the church where I spoke 'without notice' wanted to find the best of the best type of audio tape to make a copy of the message the LORD shared that night.

Months later, while I was back in California. I was on the 5 Freeway, driving from San Diego to Los Angeles. It was not an easy drive because the meeting was going to be intense. I needed a word from the LORD and the LORD was not saying anything.

After listening to me for a while, He told me to 'pull over'.

He then instructed me to put the audio tape in and listen.

I did not know what tape the LORD was talking about.

The LORD 'knowing my thoughts' told me in that moment to pull the tape out of the glove compartment.

Wow. I forgot I put the audio tape from London in the car.

I had no idea it was in the glove compartment.

Whether the LORD or His angels placed the tape there for me to pull it out in this moment or not, I was amazed to find the tape in the car!

As soon as I put the tape in the player, it was clear the message He shared through me for the people in London so long ago was exactly the message I needed to hear in this moment.

My words are just words.

His words bless to the core.

Too often, we seek words from other people instead of God.

So important to seek His truth, His words direct from Him vs. seeking the advice from anyone else.

Even if we are 'isolated' and seeking His voice, we can choose a different path based upon the news in the world. The words, the news we are bombarded with day after day, hour after hour.

## American News Influences Believers
## News Is Not Quite The News

I was privileged to work directly with the news director and senior producer of the ABC TV evening news in San Diego, California while I was focused upon my dream of becoming a TV news anchor. People repeatedly told me 'you have the voice'. So grateful they did not tell me 'you have a great voice for radio'!

Soon, I realized the dream was not turning out as I had hoped.

The news that comes in off the Associated Press wires into the news room is given a 'headline'. It is rewritten by staff writers to add impact for the 'teaser' about the evening news. Then, it is adjusted or rewritten again by the producer before the news anchor reviews the 'copy' which is adjusted again before it is shared as a news story.

Another rewrite takes place to promote the next news cast. Then, all of the notes with all of the adjustments are left for the producers to create a new headline and rewrite the same news story(ies) for the morning edition of the news without 'copying' the same headline used in prior promotion and reporting of the story.

The people viewing the news on TV told me they did not realize they were hearing the same stories merely told with different headlines throughout the day.

Now, the stories are shared moment by moment within headlines for Internet news release.

Over time, it has become a process of 'who can write the best headline' no matter what the facts are within the story so it has become 'we made you look' instead of sharing factual news. The headlines are purposely worded to grab your attention and make you read their version of details while the report is typically unrelated to the actual, factual news highlighted within the headline.

In fact, from 1982 to 1990 a man named Rich Hall made the process of re-writing and re-editing the actual news a career within his famous TV series: *Not Necessarily the News.* The show used actual news footage and he made the reality of the newsroom look comedic.

People viewing the show loved the humor while they did not realize they were actually viewing the truth about how a story is rewritten and told to grab the interest of the viewers vs. sharing the exact facts, the truth.

## Global News vs. American News

During my first trip to Europe, the LORD directed my attention to the news. The reports seemed odd. The facts were different than the reports we hear in America.

During my most recent trip to Europe, the news being reported was still warning the world about what was happening in America. The same factual reporting is as evident now as it was during my first trip to Europe. LORD keep Your hand upon us in these days!

### Lester Sumrall Training by Smith Wigglesworth

When Lester Sumrall arrived at Smith Wigglesworth's home with a newspaper under his arm Wigglesworth quickly advised Sumrall that newspapers were not allowed in his home.

Sumrall quickly placed the newspaper in the bushes by the front door before he entered Wigglesworth's home.

Wigglesworth only allowed the Bible to be read and it influenced his life, the ministry, and each of his relationships.

### Inserts: Breath of Life Moments!

Since our LORD provides each breath of life, it is important to know as you read through the 'heavy' facts He has provided within the Georgia assignment, He has prompted me to insert some paragraphs (just like this one) to help you breathe deep once again. The inserts are provided for your enjoyment and in some cases it is for your entertainment as I am often 'entertainment' for the LORD while we travel through these adventures together.

### The news.

Daily, the news tells a story from a human perspective. We are not to lean on our own human understanding.

## Christian History Was Changed 'Over Time'
## American History & Heritage Was Changed 'Over Time'
## Exactly As 'News Stories' Are Changed

Two DVDs help provide basic facts we did not know.

1. *God's Outlaw*, the true story about the life of Tyndale and what was happening in the 1500's when Tyndale translated the bible into English and arranged to smuggle copies to England.

2. *Monumental* by Kirk Cameron. The true story which we did not hear about the Pilgrims / Puritans who sacrificed everything to bring their families and the bible to America and bring us the truth about how we can retain liberty and freedom in our nation.

Pilgrims put a ban on all pagan / sun (Sunday) worship, especially the pagan celebrations of Easter (Ishtar) and Christmas (December 25, the birth date of the many – nearly all - of the gods; *gods* Dionysus was not born on December 25 so his birth date was moved to December 25). *True*

The Pilgrims arrived in America with a 500 year plan. The plan provided liberty and freedom for all during the first 250 years while they structured the colonies and arranged with the Congress and Founding Fathers to fund and distribute a bible to every family, church, and school. They were united, held peace with all Native Americans while they placed a ban on ALL pagan worship!

We have not passed on the truth from generation to generation as the LORD arranged nearly 400 years ago when He guided the Pilgrims who were Puritans, to the new land of America.

However, the plan started to fall apart in the mid-1800's and the steady decline became evident to many of the believers in other nations before it became clear to people within America.

Bottom line: We were given the truth by the Pilgrims. A lot of truth available by viewing these DVDs with family and friends!

1. The ban against pagan rituals and worship continued from 1620 to the mid-1800's, nearly 250 years.

2. Strategy of the enemy against our Christian faith and beliefs was put into place in July 1776, exactly when we gained independence from England. The development of the plan took place when the Native Americans were removed from the land in the early 1800's, the beginning of the Trail of Tears from Georgia to Oklahoma. The plan expanded each year and especially during the Civil War. The details are shared in Chapter 18, Significance of Macon, Georgia to America.

3. Then, the enemy's structure to counter our Christian faith in America was put into place when the ban was removed and the truth was 'lost in translation' with the many immigrants from nations around the world being granted land 'without taxes' if they would settle upon the land which was stolen from the Native Americans.

4. The enemy's plan was further established in each of the towns across the nation when pastors, business owners, government leaders, attorneys and judges, etc., became involved in the Masons without realizing the significance of the impact it

would have upon the community and the people; expansion of the plan began the change from America as a Republic Government to a global Democracy, as described within Chapter 18 and 19. *True*

5. Also, the enemy gained control of the nation by controlling all financial institutions as described in Chapter 19, Significance of Augusta and Jekyll Island, Georgia to America.

6. After the control measures were 'in place' regarding the finances, the enemy merely needed to put 'controls in place to take control over the people' and this plan 'sealed the fate' of America; Facts are disclosed within Chapter 20, Significance of Warm Springs, Georgia to America.

7. No matter what the enemy plots or how far the enemy has progressed upon his timeline, even scheduling a meeting in Georgia to stop a candidate who is already the people's choice in *Trump* 2016, the LORD's hand is upon His people. The believers in Christ must walk forward in FAITH for the Promises of the LORD to be fulfilled in these days. We must humble ourselves, seek His face, and turn from our wicked ways to hear from heaven! **II Chronicles 7:14.** Praying we will stand firm with our LORD because it is what we must do ***For The Sake Of America.***

Media's propaganda is believed, so making a difference in Georgia during these days is not an easy task!

Sad yet true, it is the same in each State across America!

The LORD set forth a mighty plan for me in Georgia.

*II chronicles 7:14*

I only knew about the three week trip based upon the flight ticket dates which the LORD confirmed.

It was a surprise when my time in Georgia was extended.

It was valuable time, because the LORD was revealing so much and the books were being completed and released at a rapid rate of five the first year and six the second year.

Three books were already in the editing phase of the process this year before the LORD directed all of my focus upon this message due to the fact this year is a critical election year *For The Sake Of America*.

At specific times, I questioned if my time in Georgia was complete since I was not seeing an open door.

Many in ministry were confirming that sooner or later ALL who come to Georgia to help, end up leaving without results.

It's not easy when ministry is provided at no cost and no income is arranged or offered. To me, it was starting to make sense that it was NOT going to happen 'in Georgia' especially 'in Macon'.

However, the LORD confirmed He was showing me the condition of the body of Christ in America especially through responses from the regular attending members who do not miss a Sunday, Wednesday, and often an extra Tuesday or Friday or Saturday, or all of the above. Sad status: No matter how often meetings are attended, lives are not visibly changed, people are not healed and communities are not restored.

Yikes. Just when I thought the LORD had revealed all of it about the condition of the body, it was a bigger surprise when my ministry support ended because I was extended by the LORD beyond the first year.

Each time I trusted 'it is about as much as I can accomplish' the LORD comforted me and revealed another layer of truth and confirmed He has more for me to do while 'boots on ground' in Georgia!

Since there is so much to share, I will share the layers as close to the piece by piece, step by step format the LORD provided and I'll do it within short chapters since there is a lot to take in within each, deep layer.

The facts were not told to us by our ancestors!

We did not learn these facts in school or in church!

In fact, history was 'adjusted' to be acceptable by Constantine who is credited as 'legalizing Christianity for future generations'. We have passed on the lies! The adjustments put us back to ancient times and pagan beliefs and there we remain within the church!

It's not an easy reveal but, it is 1000% necessary!

It is very clear why the LORD has confirmed what He is doing.

Revealing the truth in Georgia will hopefully result in repentance and full restoration in the region. Then, His truth will flow from Georgia across America like a mighty flood. This is His promise if we will walk forward in truth and FAITH!

Grateful to serve the LORD in these days so His truth will set the captives free from coast to coast!

The LORD sent me to Georgia with a suitcase and He insisted upon including my lap top. Without any of my reference materials or concordances, the LORD provided all of the details and new research. This confirms we serve an awesome LORD! If we will become willing to do what He wants us to do, go where He wants us to go, remain in FAITH and BELIEVE in His truth to be His representatives for the sake of the people in these unique days in our history.

As you will see within these pages, the roots are deep and they have our nation 'in limbo'. The LORD knows needs the roots need to be addressed 'in Georgia' and across this nation before His promise can be fulfilled in our lives *For The Sake Of America*.

Important: The LORD has not taken His hand off of America.

**Proverbs 3:5-6.** Trust in the Lord with all your heart,

And lean not on your own understanding;

**6** In all your ways acknowledge Him,

And He shall direct your paths.

Many prophets have declared vision and word regarding the Cyrus anointing being upon a candidate for President within the 2016 election. For the truth to be known across the nation, we need to stop waiting for God to do more!

If Christ truly lives in our hearts, our heart has not flat-lined to require revival! Restoration!

We can restore each other while we disciple and sharpen each other as iron sharpens iron when we align 'in unity' and pray as described within **II Chronicles 7:14.** *If My people who are called* *by My name will humble themselves, and pray and seek My face, and turn from their wicked ways (REPENT), then I will hear from heaven, and will forgive their sin and heal their land (RESTORE).* *O Lord . ,, And as we repent you do restore . ,,*

*We wanted future generations to be educated by the finest 'institutions'. But now we wonder why the generations have departed from church and family, faith and belief in the only true living LORD.*

We have a lot of ground to cover!

Each time the LORD gives you a special 'ah ha, so that's what happened' moment, please take a deep breath and rest a moment to let the truth soak in because our LORD has divinely orchestrated each step while I have been in Georgia for three years.

He has connected ALL of the dots!

He has 'revealed the depth of the deceit'

This is why no time is spent on the 'issues' we are facing. Our LORD has kept me focused ONLY upon the specific roots.

Here's to you for realizing **something is not right**, for being willing to gain wisdom about the deep, hidden roots in this nation.

Here's to you for realizing we have been encased in a web of deceit for so long, many within the body of Christ are unaware of who they are in Christ.

Here's to you for seeking all our LORD has prepared for those who love Him!

His promises are true. He has given us a hope and a future and His promise to the three internationally recognized prophets confirmed in vision and word is revealed now *For The Sake Of America.*

To the 3 International Recognized Prophets confirmed

# Chapter 1    For the Sake of America

Important information is shared within the introduction. If you usually skip the introduction, please turn back to page 9 and enjoy the preparation phase since the Georgia assignment was granted due to how the LORD prepared me for 'such a time as this'.

Since the information is critical to gaining understanding of our current status in America, you can trust I'll be right here, waiting for you when you are ready for Chapter 1!

## For The Sake Of America Vision

The LORD arranged for me to be 'boots on ground' in Georgia, prepared and positioned before the vision **'For The Sake Of America'** was provided. The vision was given to three internationally recognized prophets who passed away within a 12 month time frame (2014-2015) after I arrived in Georgia (2013).

## Man Shared Vision & Word From The First Prophet

The first time I heard about the vision I found the details to be amazing and I offered to pray with the man who shared the vision with me. But, while I was offering prayer he was telling me, *The vision is being shared with you 'on purpose' because the LORD told me that you are in Georgia for this purpose.*

Wow. His comment caused me to laugh because the vision is significant and would require some specific knowledge about the region which I did not have.

Personally, I thought I knew that I knew I was only going to be in Georgia for a short period of time. If the LORD had an assignment for me I trusted He would tell me why I am in Georgia before He would tell someone else.

The man was sure he was not going to be involved.

He was sure that he was supposed to release the vision and word to me.

What?

I would help the man but, take it on alone … is this possible?

## Man Shared Vision & Word From The Second Prophet

The second time I heard the details, a man said he was supposed to tell me something and as soon as he started sharing the details it sounded exactly like the same vision but the vision was given to a different prophet. This man definitely had my attention. Before I could insert anything about hearing the vision from another man, he turned to me and said the same thing, *The vision is being shared with you 'on purpose' because the LORD told me you are in Georgia for this purpose.*

No laughter this time.

Personally, I was still unaware of an assignment in Georgia for me. However, the man was sure the details of the vision and the word were supposed to be released to me. He said the LORD told him I would understand. So, I thanked the man and told him I would take it all to the LORD in prayer.

In my own insecurity, I asked if the man was going to be involved. The LORD answered quickly through the man, *You are in the region to fulfill upon the vision and word. I've prayed to know who to give it to and it is clearly the LORD's plan to release it to you and it is clear that this is not my assignment.*

LORD what?

He knows it is not his assignment.

Is it mine?

The LORD was silent.

I trusted the LORD would provide help with this, and soon.

## The LORD Sent A Third Man

# The Man Shared Vision & Word From The Third Prophet

Then, there was a third man.

This time, it felt like a 'set up' since I was not 'in a meeting'. I was attending a wedding of a very dear couple.

Individually, the bride and groom are so deep with the LORD and their first words spoken over my life were so 'right on' I was honored to be invited to witness their marriage.

After I was seated, the LORD requested I move forward two rows. It seemed odd since I am not family, but when I heard the LORD say, *Please move up two rows right now,* I moved.

A couple sat next to me within moments of the move!

Within a few minutes, the man leaned forward and said, *We need to talk after the ceremony.* No hesitation. The LORD said *Yes* through me before I took a breath to respond!

They are a very nice couple, long time friends of the groom and they said they have no plans to move to Macon, Georgia. At first, I was not quite sure why it was so important to let me know that fact. However, when he shared the exact same details of the exact same vision and word which was given to the couple by *Prophet Bob Jones* it all made sense. They confirmed the vision was given to Bob Jones when he cried out to the LORD along with two fellow prophets, *Arthur Burt from Wales and John Paul Jackson,* to know what can be done *'For The Sake Of America'.*

Not sure how long I looked like 'a deer in headlights' to him. When I could think of something to say, I asked him if he would come to Macon to assist with the process since he lives about one hour from Macon.

The words came out of my mouth before my mind clicked into gear, before I remembered his introductory statement: *No plans to ever move to Macon, Georgia.*

He was grateful the LORD confirmed it was the right time to finally release the vision and word to me. No matter what I tried to say about what the LORD had revealed since placing my feet in Macon, the man already knew the details and he was clear about his involvement with another ministry which made it impossible for him to be involved with this assignment. More facts shared about this experience and the significance of the message within 'the order of the timeline of events' in Chapter 12.

### Vision & Word Shared, Then The LORD Revealed Assignment: Georgia

Trusting you will pray with me through each of the layers of deceit as I reveal to you all the LORD has revealed to me about the plans of the enemy to keep us from living in liberty and freedom.

A lot of facts were revealed prior to receiving the vision and word, including the fact many have come to Macon, Georgia to begin the process but, sooner or later they leave.

Evidently, the LORD wanted to be sure 'no matter what the attacks are or the battles look like' I would remain 'boots on ground' in Georgia.

A lot of facts have been provided since the vision was released to me, facts which I would not have been able to comprehend if I was anywhere else in the world or America.

Within the last few days, the LORD has connected nearly all of the dots and the timing to release the vision and word to all who have ears to hear and eyes to see so their minds can begin to conceive what they have not seen or heard, what the LORD has prepared for those who love him as confirmed within **II Corinthians 2:9.**

The LORD has a special sense of humor.

This passage in scripture has been a repeated quote in every nation where He has placed my feet.

Now, after all of the equipping and training, especially during the past two and a half decades in ministry while only He knew what I needed to know to stand firm in these days *For The Sake Of America,* and I now realize His reward for me was placing my feet on the soil of the State of Georgia.

### Being In Georgia, The Deep South,
### Can Resemble Being In Another Nation

At first, the deep south truly did seem like 'another nation'. Words are used here which are clearly words known only to the people 'in the region', but now I realize the LORD knew a complete change of location would help me depart from 'being comfortable in surroundings I am fully aware of and know how to respond to terms stated'. He wanted me to come to Him as a child, for I knew not how to 'mash an elevator', nor did I know it was a real word or a phrase if someone said 'gee haw'.

In fact I had no idea how to respond since these terms were not terms I had heard before. They are real words 'in the south' of America. Both terms are Southern slang.

Mash means to push or press, 'Gee haw' actually means 'it's not working' or 'they don't get along' or 'they don't see eye to eye'.

It is tough to know what to do when the words are actually English and yet, they sound completely foreign!

The LORD has a tremendous sense of humor.

## Three Weeks Becomes Three Years

Here I was on the opposite side of the country trying to squeeze everything into three weeks.

Then, into a few more days with each group of people He introduced me to since I trusted I would only be in the region a few more days and then I would be 'going home'.

The way the LORD arranged it for me is amazing.

I'm temporary here and He arranged for me to be temporary in California. He has confirmed 'home' for me (for us) is within the family of God! He did this in other nations when seven days turns into seven extensions of seven days in a nation or while in Europe journeys to seven nations, etc. The LORD always confirmed I was in the center of the family.

This trip seemed different at first, and yet, He has arranged for me to be in the center of the family once again!

It was not reality for me until He reminded me of my statement: *I will go where You want me to go, do what You want me to do, and say what You want me to say.*

We serve an awesome LORD!

## Can One Christian Make A Difference?

The LORD knew I was clearly raised as a 'traditional Christian', advised from an early age to:

1. 'stay out of politics'.
2. 'do not mention the devil and he will leave you alone'.

Both statements were lies.

Both statements affect the status of America today.

Christians stayed out of politics.

Christians left the government structure and the decision of lawmaking up to 'other people' in the nation.

Now, Christians wonder 'what has happened to our government'?

## Significant Work To Do
## For The Sake Of America

Work was getting done 'in the region' but I was starting to feel exhausted.

So much resistance makes the days appear long.

Rare, that my energy level decreased to the point of feeling a bit weary. Unusual for me while traveling with the LORD.

### Three Years: I Thought It Was Time To Go

Without realizing it, I thought I knew nothing was going to come of all of the time in Georgia.

Therefore, I thought the LORD knew I was done and He was aligned with my plan to leave Georgia in one week.

A special couple invited me to be in the Vidalia area so I agreed to be there for one week after my trip to Alabama.

An open door was not yet evident nor a reason to remain in Georgia.

So without realizing I had slipped into a human plan, I informed God I was OK with leaving Georgia in a week after the Alabama trip.

### Alabama

The Alabama trip was special.

The plan started while I was in Columbus, Georgia.

Three days of Rodney Howard-Browne meetings.

I met a special, deep woman of God.

Prayers resulted in peace and unity in her family.

Her bible study heard the details within three days.

A woman attending was from Auburn, Alabama.

Her husband suffered a major heart attack.

Surgery was scheduled in a few days.

The man is an ordained Primitive Baptist Pastor.

He was not quite sure about a woman praying with him.

He offered a phone call to hear the prayers.

The LORD immediately declined a phone call offer.

Invitation to come to his home, day before surgery.

Doctor did not give him much hope in surviving surgery.

He spent days 'saying good-bye' to his friends.

Several hours together in prayer; his faith was restored.

Two grandfathers, both were tent pastors!

Father's side, Primitive Baptist (Lockhart) tent pastor.

Mother's side, Pentecostal (Little) tent pastor.

Seminole Indian heritage, adopted by great-grandfather.

Kathryn Kuhlman heard about his revival meetings.

She changed her return route to stop by a few nights.

She was on the platform to support him, not to preach.

Pastor regained faith and belief during our time together.

THE NEXT MORNING:

Pacemaker/Defibrillator unit inserted during surgery.

THE NEXT MORNING:

Instead of days in ICU and rehab if he survived,

He was sent home within 48 hours of the surgery.

Instead of extensive rehab and never working again,

He returned to work within a few weeks.

His testimony was shared; he invited me to preach.

The songs he recommended moments before the meeting resulted in a quick call to Vestal Goodman's Niece, Verna (Goodman) and Gerald Evans since it was clear pastor was connected with the Goodman family. The 'handwritten song book' of Rusty Goodman was filled with amazing songs which were not yet produced. The connection was so special. Grateful to be a witness. What God does because He arranges for me to show up! Meeting and friendship are a deep, long term blessing.

Since I was not seeing anything open up in Georgia yet, I prepared to leave Georgia one week after Alabama.

God knew I made a plan to leave Georgia after the invitation to be in Vidalia, Georgia for one week.

The only other person who knew about 'my thought' beyond the LORD was my mom.

Mom knew I was going to travel to Nebraska soon to visit with her because it had been close to a year since I spent time with her.

She wanted me to pack up everything in Georgia.

She trusted, since I had shared all of my human concerns and reasons with her regarding how resistant the people are and it seemed clear to me it was time for me to leave.

Sad, but true, she only heard my concerns from my human perspective. She only heard why I thought Georgia was no longer my assignment.

My concerns are almost all of the facts she heard from me so that is all she knew about 'the time in Georgia'.

Preparation took place before I went to Alabama since I have 'stuff' in Georgia due to being 'boots on ground' for three years. Hosting in America is different. People expect you will 'handle your needs'.

Linens were purchased for the beds, sheets and pillows, and towels. Winter coats and clothes which were not needed in California, along with winter scarves and sweaters. This significantly increased the wardrobe. Plus, the necessary office supplies, a printer for the lap top, books and resource materials, laundry soaps, bathroom necessities and much, much more.

A long list of 'stuff' which results in bags for each trip to each location within Georgia. It has resulted in the 'bag lady' comments because I have needed to pack different items for each location the LORD orchestrates due to the time of year and the needs for the next temporary housing option.

## Want To Make God Laugh?
## Tell Him Your Plans!

The LORD had other plans already 'laid out before me'.

Grateful our LORD has a great sense of humor!

My 'back up plan' after spending one more week in Vidalia region, still within middle-Georgia – leave!

Each time I feel 'it is time to go' – the LORD just smiles.

I've not been sure of the timing.

It might be another week, a month or more but, no door appeared to be open when I left Macon for Alabama so I trusted it was time for me to leave Georgia!

### Christ Felt The Same Way!

The LORD reminded me of the ministry of Christ. Some trust it was three years and some scholars say 70 weeks. It was feeling the same for me whether it has been the 1.5 years with a car or including the 1.5 years without a car.

Each time I felt I was hitting a brick wall, I trusted I had reached the point Christ reached as confirmed in **Matthew 17:17, Mark 9:19m and Luke 9:41.** All three references are identical with the LORD telling the disciples they were not getting what He was teaching so He inquired how long must He be with them for they are a perverse, faithless and unbelieving generation.

### Silly Me, I Shared My Complaint With The LORD

Feeling like 'all effort is for naught' in the middle-Georgia region especially since I remained for two years beyond the point of receiving a copy of 20 year old Graham Cooke word on unity for Macon. God sent him to Macon the first time He was sent to America. Graham's word was not addressed or proceeded upon by the key leaders who were in the meeting or the ones who received a copy of the word. They knew it was from the LORD but, even though the word declared it was critical for the region to proceed within 5-10 years to unite the believers, nothing was done in more than 20 years. Now, they are questioning and attacking me about unity!

### Christ Felt The Same Way!

When I stated my complaints, I confirmed the people love hearing the details about Graham's word but then, they speak against the plan and me!

While in the midst of my 'pity party' the LORD reminded me of the devout members of the synagogue who challenged Christ when He first expressed wisdom in their presence. They trusted it was not possible at his young age but, He continued to share wisdom everywhere with everyone.

### Paul Felt The Same Way!

Plus, it was the devout members of the fellowship who were the ones gathering and aligning together in their plan to stone Paul and leave him for dead outside the city gate, but the LORD resurrected Paul and transported him to another city to preach the truth.

### The LORD Resurrects

Wow. The LORD had my attention. I've not been stoned.

Before I could fully take it all in, the LORD provided another example.

On Palm Sunday, the public, the people honored Christ, waved palm branches as he was paraded through the streets. They stated and sang praises to him.

Before the end of the week, the devout members of the fellowship cried out, *Crucify Him!*

Wow. I've not been persecuted. I've not been crucified.

Before I could take it all in, the LORD confirmed Christ was resurrected and continued to bring truth to the people!

The LORD was preparing me for the change of plans!

I felt the assignment was 'dead'.

What I did not know is our LORD was resurrecting me, transporting me to a new region within middle-Georgia, and He was resurrecting the assignment to continue until the truth is provided to the people!

**Here to Serve**
**Even if it Seems Like it is**
**Only for the LORD's Entertainment!**

The day after I arrived to spend a week with a couple who invited me to be in the Vidalia region of Georgia, the car donated to my ministry overheated.

The car had just entered the gate of the city.

Now, the car was dead!

Since the car would not 'hold water' it had to be towed.

Intense prayers before the tow truck arrived!

The initial estimate from a local mechanic was $1500 if only labor and parts to repair the car were required. If engine required replacement the cost would be closer to $2000.

My prayers were human based, thoughts linked to my own 'in my head' back-up plan vs. the plan the LORD was orchestrating, a plan which He had not revealed to me, yet: *How can I leave Georgia now if I do not have a car to 'load all of my stuff' & go?*

Quiet time with the LORD was needed because I had no idea what His next step for me would require.

What did I find out?

One of my best talents is still making the LORD laugh!

The mechanic I was referred to was dumbfounded. He said it was impossible for the car to overheat in less than ten miles.

My next prayers, prayers which should have been my first prayers: *Show me Your truth LORD!*

As much as I appreciate the opportunity to re-encourage pastors, the opportunity to participate in the restoration of a life and a family is absolutely as rewarding for me to witness.

In the midst of assisting with the restoration process of lives and ministries in the region, the LORD provided the following statistic: *18 hangings within the two county area during the year where He placed my feet for one week, plus due to car repairs.*

There is much to do in many regions across our nation while I have to stand upon the promise from the LORD that what He is doing in Georgia in these days will restore the region and what He reveals to the people will flow across America as a mighty flood.

He said it. I am standing upon it in faith because I believe it!

My next prayers: *Thank you LORD for Your provision, for Your resolution for the car, for Your wisdom, and a sign from You to let me know Your timing to take the next step.*

Many of my repentance prayers are for speaking 'my truth' to the LORD before I realize my words have no value within His plan and my plans merely cause the LORD to laugh!

As soon as I was 're-aligned' with the LORD's plan, He reminded me of the prophetic word shared long ago by a major prophet in America, a word confirmed by a young boy in Australia when the LORD prompted him to draw a picture of a mouse clinging on to the back of the elephant.

The prophet said, *The LORD showed me you in a vision as the mouse to the elephant. You are biting the ankle and screaming to make the elephant move.*

*Then, you are running up and swinging on the tail and screaming.*

*Then, you are yelling in the left ear and biting the ear. Then, you run to the right ear. You are biting the ear and screaming in the right ear until the elephant finally moves!*

When the prophet said the elephant is the body of Christ, I had tears. Then, he said, *Since you are willing to be persistent and tireless* (indefatigable means tireless, persistent) *in your pursuit, it may take years but, sooner or later the body of Christ will move!*

The result of the prayers and the steps revealed are provided in this book.

The sleeping church is waking up!

I'm grateful!

He forgives me and I am grateful for the opportunity to share the truth with you as our LORD has shared it with me during the mighty adventures the LORD has arranged in my life. I now know how critical it is for me to stand firm and remain 'boots on ground' in Georgia to fulfill upon *'The Georgia Assignment: For The Sake Of America'!*

## Chapter 2    Seeing America Through God's Eyes

**Opening Scene:** Angels strategically positioned across the nation from sea to sea while the song *America the Beautiful* is playing softly in the background and as the volume increases, bright lights reveal warring angels with swords along the borders on the north and the south protecting the nation as ONE NATION UNDER GOD appears across the flag waving on screen.

**Truth:** The LORD does dispatch His angels for our sake while the drama expressed in a movie scene becomes easier for us to comprehend than the truth within the scriptures. Ouch!

**Psalm 91:11.** *For He shall give His angels charge over you, to keep you in all your ways.*

## Caution: Do Not Become Earthly / Worldly Focused

Can we hear the truth without being entertained?

Can we set aside all news sources 'in the world' and seek the answers from the only living LORD?

## Current Generations Unaware of the Truth

A young man shared his summary of life with me last week.

It was fascinating to hear a brand new view on life.

He said, *All religions want to do good works in the world so they are all the same. It does not matter which one you choose or if you choose one just do good works during your life.*

Without a thought, the LORD prompted me to laugh so hard it surprised the young man as much as it surprised me!

He asked if I was OK. I nodded.

Then, the LORD took over and the words that came out of my mouth blessed me and opened his heart and mind to hear the truth while I was still laughing: *All of their gods are dead!*

The young man was surprised. I was still laughing while the LORD continued, *The only true living LORD is the only one I serve. There is a difference. All of the other gods are dead! It is not about our good works. We cannot do enough 'good works' to obtain the grace and mercy of the only living LORD.*

The young man was shocked.

He was quiet because he was completely stunned.

He had a deeper question to answer than he imagined.

When he spoke, he confirmed the world influenced him to stop being in fellowship with any Christians, including his own family. The youth leaders, husband and wife, argued constantly and obtained a divorce shortly after he joined the youth group. Then, they left the church. It impacted his view of the body of Christ!

He learned within his college education to be politically correct and not make a statement which would offend any other religion.

He did not realize the offense against dead gods does not have any impact upon anything because they are all dead!

## Only Christians Have Power & Authority

### Because Christ Resides in Our Hearts!

The power within Christians is very different because Christ resides in our heart and the power within us is 'resurrection power' which is a greater power than anything that anyone could produce in the world based upon their own strength!

**1 John 4:4.** *You are of God, little children, and have overcome them, because He who is in you is greater than he who is in the world.*

The young man was in tears.

He wants to have more conversation again, soon. We will.

He knew I was merely stopping for a cup of coffee on my way to another region but, we can stay in touch and I will answer any questions while he regains his faith and belief in the only true living LORD.

### Our faith escorts us into the LORD's promise!

It's sad, but true. This young man's response is the typical response from people across the nation who have become influenced by becoming powerful and successful in the world.

They have gained enough income, assets, and standing in the community to feel all is fine. They are unaware, this is the lie!

This is exactly where my life was when the LORD took my hand and showed me who I am through His eyes.

He showed me it is impossible to please all of the people all of the time but, we are trained to be independent through the education system.

The more educated, the more independent.

In fact, I learned the world system very well since it was what made me 'appear successful and wealthy' and that appearance is what resulted in acceptance throughout the region. I was so deep in the 'world education on how to be successful' process I had a plan for everything. I had my retirement figured out and I was doing it 'all by myself' since the world process had destroyed me to the point I could not function in daily life!

The facts are briefly provided within my book *Nation Restoration.* The book also describes the identity theft crimes we are dealing with across America since I had the opportunity to experience the most extreme cases while I was moved on to new Social Security numbers frequently by the agents investigating the Superior Court Judges and attorneys who were finally sentenced to prison on Federal RICO (racketeering) charges.

Life was so full, there are times and people I do not remember. The wealth I accumulated was stolen over and over again. Since I was good at 'rebuilding', it took a good dose of what the world can do to a woman of God for me to realize it was never going to happen 'in the world' since the world is not my source, my provider, or my friend.

In any moment, even after ALL my LORD has done for me, if I'm not diligent and obedient, my human thoughts can easily align with the tactics of the enemy which would put me into: <u>fear, doubt and unbelief</u>. At that point, it's easy for the enemy to <u>steal, kill and destroy</u>!

In fact, it happened again before the LORD prompted me to prepare this book. Remember, I'm the one who declared: *If I do not have the funds or the car to drive then I am done.* That is the lie. I had to get my mind back to the truth of the word!

The LORD answered my prayer quickly when I asked, *What do you want from me?*

Since I learned a lot while gaining college degrees and certifications, etc., I laid out all of the projects which represented 'my labor'.

Not sure how long I sat there waiting for the LORD to identify which one was the one He wanted me to focus upon. In fact, I sat there for so long I think I actually drifted off to sleep since I had not participated in an 'open vision' prior to this night.

The LORD gained my attention when a funnel appeared. It was a large funnel. I was staring at the bottom of the funnel to see exactly what God was going to show me, as God scooped up all of the papers and inserted them into the funnel. But as soon as the funnel was filled with all of my stuff, God merely tapped the small end of the funnel and all of the papers fell in all directions.

As I watched the projects flying through the air I realized no specific task was being identified and I did not even realize God put His hand through the small end of the funnel until I saw God pull me through.

It was a shock to watch what appeared to be a movie of my life with God picking me up. All God had in His hand was me. I was so human in that moment, plus I was confused because not one topic appeared among the papers so I asked, *"What do you want from me?"* And the Holy Spirit softly confirmed when I saw God's hand lift me up higher in the air, *"What I want is you."*

It was a humbling experience. I had no idea what God could do with me. I was in tears as God showed me a second vision. I was on a platform with Him and the floodlights on the stage were shining bright. God made it a familiar experience as it was exactly what I experience as a conference speaker. It was even more exciting because I recognized all of the people in the first row.

God said, *"You are here for them."* I told God it was not very much to fill my life by being here for the people I already know. As I said this, God turned the floodlights to shine upon the multitude which stretched out across the land in all directions. I immediately confirmed I did not know any of these people, however, God said, *"Because you blessed the ones you know, they blessed the rest."*

I was in awe and I was embarrassed. To me, this sounded rather lofty. God knew my concern and He immediately showed me a third vision. God turned the view so He could show me His perspective from my side profile. He showed me the letters of my words leaving my lips and going out to the front row and then bouncing throughout the multitude. *3rd Vision*

I was in awe as God showed me how His words were leaving my mouth and traveling to the heart of the first person and on to the next and the next, on and on until they reached the multitude.

It appeared the same to me as a stone does when it is cast upon the water and it touches the water many times while it skips across a lake. God knew I used to try and make stones skip across the water with cousins when I was young so God used that analogy and it made sense to me. However, I still felt I was incapable of being a representative for God, an Ambassador for Christ.

Since the LORD can take me from being a pew warming Lutheran to representing Him wherever He places my feet upon the soil, I know He can do it with you! All He wants is you!

America is in trouble. God needs you to stand firm!

The Body of Christ is in trouble. God needs you to stand firm!

When I was left without the 'promise / the blessing' by a powerful man of God (the one who shared the mouse to the elephant word), my gas tank was full and I had no way to get gas or pay for the rental car. The LORD filled the tank, gave me a word: *"Not enough of my men are preparing and putting on their steel toed boots to march with Me, so I am having to call forth my women, even my widows and my orphans, to prepare my Army to march with Me before the SONrise."*

The LORD kept the gas tank full while He sent me to meetings I knew nothing about when the car was rented. He arranged for a man to hand me an envelope to pay the rental car for five weeks vs. the one week the man offered. The LORD was in the process of arranging all details for me to be in Africa in three weeks after the man brought the envelope which paid the rental car until my departure flight to Africa.

Will you prepare, put on your steel toed boots and march with the LORD in these days before the SONrise?

Since you are now 'armed with the truth', I trust you will!

## Chapter 3     Georgia on God's Mind

Georgia was NOT on my mind!

A funny thing happened after spending three summer days with a host family in Macon, Georgia during June 2013.

My host was introduced to me during a full week of celebration due to the LORD sending me to be His witness for the coronation of a King in Ghana, West Africa.

The two adult children living in the home said three days are not enough time to really get to know Macon so I needed to plan on staying three weeks next time.

Sounded funny.

No idea what they were talking about.

In my mind, there was no 'next time' on my calendar.

In fact, there were no plans to return to Macon.

However, in about three months the LORD arranged another flight after He confirmed the dates and exactly what I was supposed to pack for a three week return trip to Macon, Georgia.

Hesitant about packing my lap top since I knew the family was focused upon introducing me to more BBQ locations and tourist sights in the area in June. Therefore, I trusted I was taking a break from the computer for a while. Exciting since it would be a first vacation in more than two decades!

Vacation? Little did I know vacation was NOT on God's mind!

The LORD insisted the lap top needed to travel with me for the three week trip. On board a flight to Atlanta with 'lap top' in hand.

## Requirement: 'Boots on Ground' in Georgia

Only the LORD knew this trip would turn into a major adventure in Georgia.

That's right. Georgia time was clearly a secret with the LORD even after I was 'boots on ground' in Macon!

Now, three years have flown by while the LORD has revealed so much truth and history I did not know. It is absolutely amazing.

In fact, the LORD has provided so much truth it is difficult to explain in conversation even with the people who reside in Georgia and know they are hear for a purpose.

It is especially hard to explain to the people who want the LORD 'to do more' ... 'to do it all'. They are clearly unaware 'He does even more through us in these days than He did while He was here on earth', 'He knew we could do it all and more because He sent the Holy Spirit' and 'we are a special part of it all'.

Often I hear people say, *I'm not to worry about it ... the LORD will do what the LORD wants to do about it.*

Yikes! Are they not willing to hear what the LORD wants them to do? Many 'in church' are unaware we are to see to the needs of the widows and the orphans! We need to wake up!

It baffles me since the LORD sent us to earth to do His will and as Christ confirmed the truth within the Lord's prayer which He taught us to pray, **Matthew 6:9-13**. Doing exactly what the LORD wants us to do and saying what the LORD wants us to say is often missing!

In fact, most of what the LORD said I need to know about Georgia is not known by people who have lived in Georgia for three or four decades or their lifetime.

It has been a shock at each phase of this journey due to the fact Georgians are hearing the facts from me for the first time in their life, exactly as I am hearing it for the first time from the LORD.

Why do I hear it directly? I actually told the LORD:

**I Will Go Where You Want Me To Go**
**I Will Do What You Want Me To Do**
**I Will Say What You Want Me To Say**

The little return trip for exactly three weeks has become a journey with the LORD which has been a major adventure to say the least! His focus has clearly been 'all about Georgia'.

Only the LORD knew I needed to be 'boots on ground' to see what He wanted me to see, so He could show me how and when to do what He wanted me to do.

People have told me the job is too big for one person.

It's OK with me because it's God's job. I just have to show up!

In the midst of prayer, a prophetic vision was given to me by the LORD which confirmed it is 'all about Georgia, *For The Sake Of America'*. Wow! We serve an awesome LORD!

## Step By Step

Since we have a lot of ground to cover and the LORD only gives us as much of His presence and wisdom as I (we) can handle at any given time, I will share this journey with you exactly as our LORD has divinely orchestrated the 'reveal' moments with me since the truth is His ways are definitely far better than ours (mine) and they are everlasting!

## In the Beginning: Three Weeks in Georgia

In the beginning, I was invited to speak in the region and I was prompted to share a few details about what the LORD does through me when He places my feet upon the soil of a nation.

It was not part of my thinking or my personal plan that the LORD was setting forth a foundation for my feet to be placed on the soil of a different part of our nation, in America, to do and say what He would have me do and say in Georgia!

When the specific dates were arranged, tours of the area and trips to BBQ locations, cotton fields, pecan and peach orchards expanded throughout the region.

At the same time, I was invited to preach more often since I was 'in town' for three weeks this time. The LORD expressed an urgency each time for me to share more facts with the people than I shared during the brief three day visit, three months prior.

Due to the tight time frame arranged, I trusted I was doing everything I could think of to help squeeze everything the LORD has given to me into the preaching invitations and sharing with the people during local home fellowship meetings within three weeks!

Immediately, the people were hearing deep truth and they were sure I was bringing revival to their region. So, the people started to introduce me to the key pastors and ministries because I was very clear about my flight date which meant I was leaving in a few days.

## Revival Claim

### Through me, LORD!

One pastor heard I was going to attend the service. He told the people of a vision the LORD showed him many years before that it was planned by the LORD for him to be the one in the region to usher in the revival. It would come in through him slowly and it would go out through him slowly.

What? Come in and go out slowly?

This did not make any sense to me.

Ushering in the revival, great. But, slowly coming in and knowing it would go out slowly seemed quite odd.

He asked for 50 people to provide financial and prayer support for the revival by submitting their financial support and confirming their commitment of support through the church Facebook page.

Due to the request to communicate through Facebook, I did submit my questions. Due to no response, I sent a personal message to the pastor on Facebook. I told him a little bit about me and I asked him if we could meet about what the LORD was stating regarding revival coming slowly into the region and then going out slowly.

My message did not receive a response at that time or since.


**Through a servant of the LORD!**

Plans to cook a holiday meal for a family quickly changed.

The woman informed me once I was in her car that the LORD changed the plans.

She said the new plans meant we were headed to Nashville.

I quickly called the host family. They trusted I would not be back for a couple of days since they thought I was headed to Nashville, Tennessee. However, there is a Nashville, Georgia and we were on our way south to meet a special servant of the LORD.

This is all I knew until I entered into the home of a mighty woman of God!

The peace, the depth of wisdom shared in brief moments when she was available were evident even though she was fully involved hosting a holiday meal for the founders and the residents of the House of Hope.

In awe while I observed the beautiful young women around the table who committed to a year of recovery away from their families. The testimonies they shared were amazing.

Life in Georgia changed for me in that moment.

One of the young ladies just returned from a lengthy internship with Heidi Baker. We gained a close friendship the moment we met.

As a witness to the depth of fellowship and honoring of the women who have overcome their circumstances, there was nothing else required of me beyond observing what was taking place in the home of Rebecca King, a home the LORD named *The House of David.*

Rebecca's team stated she holds a weekly bible study every Wednesday.

The woman who invited me to go along to Nashville that day drove me to the bible study each Wednesday (except for two extremely unusual ice and snow storm days) for the next two months.

A deep honor to sit in the midst of a corporate environment where the depth of truth was so evident I needed to keep an extra stack of Kleenex stuffed in my purse to get through the six hours of bible study and fellowship time.

When the truth is so deep, it is not easy to share the experience with people who are OK with the status quo or they believe 'a little dab will do ya'!

Between the hosting families, the drivers (since my car was at a friend's home near the airport in San Diego, California) and each one the LORD sent to me during these days, the LORD was revealing the condition of the body of Christ from all angles and through the hearts and minds of people representing all ages!

## Chapter 4    Open the Lap Top and Type!

Before the LORD revealed the fact He was going to make Georgia an assignment, He prompted me to prepare the first three books of the many released. He has prompted me to prepare several while I've been in Georgia. A dozen are complete and three more books are 'in the editing process' while this book is being edited and released.

However, the LORD has confirmed the timing is urgent to release the visions and words He has shared *For The Sake Of America* so this book has become His priority and it is being pushed through to the head of the publishing line!

The trilogy I trusted would be the 'entire set of books' are:

*1. It's A Faith Walk!* covers about seven months of a three year journey with only enough time at home to do laundry and re-pack for the next assignment in a different part of the world. Details were orchestrated by the LORD while I did not have a car, a phone, a bank or credit account.

**Invited:** The divine orchestration of details resulted in invitations to speak throughout the region.

**Challenged:** The majority of invitations included the requirement to 'not speak about the Holy Spirit or include the Holy Spirit within the details'. *Unreal,*

**Declined:** Easy decision. Denying the Holy Spirit is denying the word and guidance from the Father and Christ. *True*

**If the Holy Spirit is not welcome, there is nothing for me to say**! There is nothing I can do or say to explain the mighty orchestration that only the LORD can arrange on my behalf. Only the LORD could send me to the various nations without an extra coin or tunic, set me before governors and kings and ensure me that I will be home safe after the journey without a concern about provision or security. *Wow* *True*

**Challenged:** Informed by many it would not be God sending me nation to nation since He only sends 'two' at a time, not one. Therefore, I am a 'lone ranger' in the body and that's not good.

**The LORD:** Provided the truth before I went into my 'they are doing it again speech. *Did I send two tickets to Australia ... Africa ... London ... the Kingdom of Tonga ... Denmark ...*

*Norway ... Sweden ... or did I send one? They are not questioning you, they are questioning Me and what I can do with and for you. Witnesses were provided in every nation ... because you agreed to go in My name.*

The LORD confirmed when He sent me to Newcastle, England **In Search of Wigglesworth** that He sent two witnesses and they were in awe of each detail during every moment of the journey and they were sharing the truth far and wide until they returned to their local prayer and fellowship groups. When they were questioned about the magnificent orchestration, they were not believed so they denied in part or in whole everything the LORD orchestrated regarding each of the details during each step of the journey.

The LORD confirmed again, He was able to do the same with Wigglesworth since without cars, phones, debit or credit cards and He can position me much quicker since He had to send Wigglesworth by boat due to no planes!

Our LORD keeps His message simple!

2. ***God's Storehouse Principle***. Plus, ***God's Storehouse Principle* workbook.** His Storehouse Principle became the theme when I was invited to preach. The Storehouse Principle helps us fulfill upon the LORD's request to 'feed my lambs', especially see to the needs of the widows and the orphans.

**Challenged:** How can you speak about ministry and the church when your immediate family are not ordained pastors?

**The LORD:** Provided the response immediately. My family is filled with pastors, both my ancestors and relatives in the current generations.

Methodist missionaries in the Congo/Zaire/Congo for 44 years, Mission Aviation Fellowship pastor and pilot providing supplies throughout Brazil and beyond for a few decades, along with Lutheran and Presbyterian pastors.

The LORD prompted me to not respond as it is not important about the perspective of man upon ministry, it is important to our LORD if we will serve and align with His truth and will, His plans and purpose for these days. We are not on earth to align with man.


*3. God's Currency.* Due to the critical days we are living in with the pending collapse of one or more currencies and entire nations going bankrupt, the LORD prompted me to prepare the third book.

He spoke the two words of the title through me when David and Polly Crawford, hosts of a local cable TV program, **The Word of God,** asked a simple question: *Why has God placed you in Macon, Georgia?* It was not evident on my face while viewing the DVD of the interview segment however, I was in a serious conversation with our LORD. What came out of my mouth was a surprise to me!

He reminded me of His answer when He confirmed the book title for it is His desire for us to become a separate and set apart people, a peculiar people, a holy nation, filled with faith, functioning in His storehouse principle and operating within His currency. The only way to proceed is based upon how the LORD has arranged for us to live in the world within His currency and His provision so no matter what the government or the world decide to do it will not affect us within the Body of Christ. *Yes Lord*

He brought the message home for this Holm while sending me to London (seven) times within twelve months. Departing America with a five dollar bill each time and no matter how long I was away from America, and no matter how many nations I was invited to and currencies were exchanged while I was away, upon my return to America my wallet included a five dollar bill. I found it odd and a bit funny but, the LORD quickly confirmed: ***I'm training you to live on My currency instead of the currency of a nation.***

Why is all of this so important?

We were never to be part of 'the world plan', lean upon human understanding and be affected by the daily and hourly news reports! We were not to become dependent upon the decisions of a national government or world leaders.

We are to be a peculiar people, a holy nation!

Oh, if we could see each other as being peculiar because we are His and love each other for the many reasons He loves each of us!

Hope you realize, I'm not perfect regarding these lessons!

After London, I was still 'in training' when I only had $20 remaining in my wallet to fill the tank after church. There was a special gas station with the lowest prices in town near Bishop McKinney's St. Stephen's Cathedral. The LORD knew a presentation regarding mission work was going to request a donation to continue their work.

The LORD prompted me to give the ministry the $20 bill in my wallet. It was all the cash I had with me to get the tank of gas so I resisted but, the LORD insisted.

The $20 was donated and a sealed envelope with ministry materials was handed to me.

After I left the church, the LORD prompted me to open the sealed envelope. To my surprise a crisp, new $20 bill was inside.

I ran back to the leader of the ministry and asked if they had inserted anything into the envelope beyond the ministry materials. The team members confirmed the envelopes are filled and sealed by a production company and not by their ministry. Therefore, only their materials were inserted in the envelope.

As I walked back to my car, the LORD reminded me that He was interested in my obedience. In this moment it became clear He had an angel standing by to provide the $20 inside a sealed envelope!

Provision for me was arranged, His blessing came to me because I was obedient.

**Sharing the truth far and wide.**

The search for deep people to share the Rebecca King bible study with resulted in the introduction of several people in Macon to a bible study in Nashville, Georgia.

One couple enjoyed the details so much while I was attending a local fellowship, they invited me to attend a tent ministry which was described as a close team equipped and trained for revival.

**Revival through our ministry, LORD!**

Tent ministry trusted the revival would happen specifically through them for the region.

Within a few days, I was personally introduced to a tent ministry in the region which met in personal homes. I trusted they operated as a home based church which held tent meetings when prompted by the LORD. This is a great concept.

They knew the LORD was going to bring revival to the region through them and they said it would begin within the inner city and move outward vs. from the churches in the suburbs and move into the city. Again, I was finding it odd to hear the restraints regarding how the LORD will do what the LORD wants to do.

Since I did not have a permanent location or a vehicle at that time they offered for me to have a place to live and transportation if I would become an exclusive covenant member of their fellowship. They were clear that they not looking for 'members'.

The two founders confirmed they are in a covenant agreement until death (instead of to life). Stunned.

The LORD was already speaking to me about this structure before the meeting concluded. However, it was not easy to provide input since the men were sure they were supposed to offer an option to provide for me after I fully submitted to their leadership.

They confirmed when I become part of the exclusive covenant agreement under their leadership team, they will be sure I have a ride to get to their church and I will have a place to live.

Wow. This sounded more like an exclusive group vs. a true gathering of the believers.

This status was an eye opener for me within the body of Christ!

## Family, Christians, Joint Heirs with Christ

The LORD was prompting me to be available in the region to unite the believers and in that capacity, which I fully explained to the two men, I was not able to become an exclusive covenant family member with one fellowship. I also explained my provision comes from the LORD and I belong to the LORD. Plus, I spent some time confirming how the LORD has established the family of believers as an 'inclusive' fellowship of ALL who will choose Christ.

The family of the body of Christ includes ALL who come by His invitation confirmed in the King James Version, **Revelation 22:17.** *...whosoever will, come.* The family of the LORD is described in **Matthew 12:50.** *For whosoever shall do the will of my Father which is in heaven, the same is my brother, and sister and mother.* Family is confirmed again in **Mark 3:35.**

## We Are Christians

## Understanding Or Knowledge Alone Is Not Enough

## Wisdom Requires Gaining Knowledge And Understanding

The LORD has a tremendous sense of humor.

I was raised in a community with Scandinavian Lutherans and German Catholics. We wanted all people to know the truth and the truth which was taught to us as children: *become good Lutherans.*

So when I met people who did not go to church, I invited them to become Lutherans. It made sense because it was what I knew.

Every Sunday Reverend Leverson would be in the flowing white robes with the appropriate color of the vestment for the church calendar and he would follow the acolyte dressed in a long white robe, carrying the Lutheran flag and a tall ornate cross.

Tears flowed while we stood up and I heard the people sing the same hymn at the beginning of every Sunday morning service:

1. Holy, holy, holy! Lord God Almighty!
Early in the morning our song shall rise to thee.
Holy, holy, holy! Merciful and mighty,

God in three persons, blessed Trinity!

2. Holy, holy, holy! All the saints adore thee,
Casting down their golden crowns around the glassy sea;
Cherubim and seraphim falling down before thee,
Which wert, and art, and evermore shalt be.

3. Holy, holy, holy! Though the darkness hide thee,
Though the eye of sinful man thy glory may not see,
Only thou art holy; there is none beside thee,
Perfect in power, in love and purity.

4. Holy, holy, holy! Lord God Almighty!
All thy works shall praise thy name, in earth and sky and sea.
Holy, holy, holy! Merciful and mighty,
God in three persons, blessed Trinity.


As Lutheran as I became, the above song was actually found on line with the copy confirmation from a page out of a Methodist hymnal.

As believers, we are more alike than we are different!

However, we have separated from each other due to denominations.

If we are 'in Christ' we are all brothers and sisters!

When, I moved from Nebraska to California and the Scandinavians I met were Catholic and the Germans were Lutheran, life seemed a bit confusing.

This change from 'all I knew' was not easy to reconcile!

**Truth:** We are more alike than we are different!

If we are 'in Christ' we are all brothers and sisters!

The Corinthians were merely ALL believers in Corinth.

The Ephesians were ALL of the believers in their region.

Same for the Philippians.

Can you imagine what it would be like if ALL Christians in each region united together for we are all followers of Christ and therefore the resurrection power and authority is 'in us' so when we gather two or more together He is in the midst!

LORD help us unite together and stand firm in Your truth so ALL of the dis-eases and lies are removed while we gather and sharpen each other in Your truth as iron sharpens iron!

The LORD knows I have not made His job easy with me since I trusted it was His plan for me to learn 'how to be a good Lutheran' while He has absolutely reminded me who I am with Him and who I was when I was 'in confusion': *I was merely living my life as a good pew warmer!*

The LORD has opened my eyes to the truth as only He can!

May we all be able to give up being a pew warmer!

The LORD was clear when I shared extensive truth from the LORD with a man in Macon, Georgia who stated with great conviction: *You need to understand with my 40 years of Christian education you are not going to be able to tell me anything.*

This statement required more face time with our LORD.

The LORD confirmed the man was speaking to Him and not to me. The man was not going to accept anything the LORD had to say. Therefore, there was nothing to say because the man could not hear anything from the LORD. I was merely His representative.

Tears ... Holy Spirit (fall over the bottom lid) tears.

The LORD reminded me about my time 'in training with Him' and how I was 'in training' by becoming a rally driver.

It was a very unique time in my life, driving on freeways in California vs. the highways in Nebraska!

A little 'practice' would help.

Friends mentioned the rally club in San Diego. However, it was a 'drive on a track' club. Most drivers had amazing sports cars compared to my Nissan Z while the track did not seem like a good challenge.

The Santa Barbara rally club conducts two 'moonlight' rallies from 10:30 PM to 10:30 AM in June and December. Their rally is a high speed (averaging 55 miles per hour) competition through California mountain routes from Santa Barbara to either Palm Springs or Las Vegas.

The challenge of navigating on mountain roads during the middle of the night made driving on California freeways much easier.

A lot of the training the LORD has arranged is similar to the level of challenges provided within a rally race and by well-meaning Christians who do not seek the response of the LORD first.

May we seek the truth from the LORD before we challenge what the LORD is doing in and through His people in these days.

May we remain open to His truth all of our days! May we come to the Father in awe and wonder as His little children! It's a beautiful thing to come to Him with that level of joy ready to receive His truth and tireless love for us!

## Chapter 5      Confirmation Unity Is Possible

The books were released.

Temporary housing option was coming to a close.

Ministry support stopped.

Requested confirmation from someone who does not know me, a confirmation which clearly comes from the LORD.

To my surprise, a family invited me to a new fellowship location for Sunday worship the next day.

It was an amazing fellowship. The music helped everyone enter into deep worship. Grateful!

Then, it happened.

A woman grabbed the microphone. She said, *Someone needs to hear from the LORD that He has placed you in this region for*

***His purpose.*** Not sure how long I stopped breathing since the woman continued to share the specifics and I only know a couple of them!

She proceeded with the word, ***As the LORD moved Abraham away from his family and his region, the LORD has moved you.***

**Promises to Abram**

**Genesis 12:1-3.**

Now the Lord had said to Abram:

***"Get out of your country,***

***From your family***

***And from your father's house,***

***To a land that I will show you.***

***2 I will make you a great nation;***

***I will bless you***

***And make your name great;***

***And you shall be a blessing.***

***3 I will bless those who bless you,***

***And I will curse him who curses you;***

***And in you all the families of the earth shall be blessed."***

The LORD knows I have always stated it matters not if the people remember my name. What does matter is that they remember a woman was sent their way and since that day, their life will never be the same.

The woman continued to share the word, *As it was for Naomi and Ruth … challenges came when Naomi went to another land but, when her time was finished and she returned to those she knew, Ruth went with her and they were blessed.* **Ruth 1 and 2.**

The night before the move, about 11 PM, an offer was extended for me to move to the next temporary location. Grateful.

Challenges were presented immediately and there were many.

The LORD was not speaking about my return to 'a home location'. In fact. as I prayed, instead of hearing any details about a plan for my return to what was familiar, He focused my attention upon the deep issues in the region plus, the orphans and the widows. Ah, it's all about 'feed my lambs'!


### What Will It Take For The People To Unite?


On the verge of asking if the LORD had an assignment somewhere else for me since I was needing a location He identified as my next location, again.

He immediately arranged an invitation to a local fellowship meeting to meet a prophet, Nancy Haney from Alaska. Nancy was the speaker and many in the region knew her due to meetings held twice a year the prior five years.

It was the first time I heard Nancy speak. At the end of the meeting, she had a specific word for me: *I see circles and circles and circles, like you are busy, you drink and you draw from one circle to the other, and that's what you do, you drink and draw and you bring these circles together. You are going to be pulling many groups together. All these groups need each other and He is going to use you for you have ears to hear and you hear His deep truth. You are filtering what is nonsense and what is real. He is going to sharpen that even more. You are going to give favor in circles, people are going to call you and want to know what you know about that circle, because you have been in that circle, and because of what you say they are going to merge. It is going to expand, become bigger than you could imagine. God has never given me this word before. I see circles and circles and circles. God sees He is the apple in your eye. You have made him the apple of your eye. God's favor on finances, health, relationships, circles upon circles in the name of Jesus ..favor favor favor.*

Re-encouraged!

This is how it progressed throughout the region. I was new to the area and yet, I was the one introducing people in the region to people they needed to connect with in the various fellowship groups, people they had not met, yet.

This word confirmed unity is possible. So, I thanked the LORD again for directing my steps.

**Moravian Falls, Prayer Mountain**

Early the next morning eight powerful women of God embarked on a journey to the special location of Prayer Mountain at Moravian Falls, North Carolina.

Each prayer while on the mountain top was answered within the same moments.

Friends confirmed this fact through their testimonies as soon as I was back in Macon. Powerful to be in an environment where the body of Christ is united together in prayer!

## Rebecca King and Rick Tenner

### Sid Roth Interview, It's Supernatural

An amazing day. The LORD has a tremendous sense of humor. When He prompted me to insert faith based quotes in *It's A Faith Walk!* the year before He directed my attention to so many quotes by Rick Renner I actually cried out to the LORD to remind Him this is NOT Rick's book!

Now, the LORD has arranged for me to actually hear Rick Renner's testimony 'in person'. Powerful!

Dr. Nancy Franklin met me for the first time when I handed her a reserved seat ticket for the interview of Rebecca King and Rick Renner by Sid Roth on It's Supernatural.

Dr Franklin's first words to me after shaking my hand were a complete surprise: *Thank you God for answering my prayers by*

81

*sending Your apostle to Macon to unite the believers ... let me know how I can help.*

Standing in awe due to hearing another confirmation, needless to say I was 'on cloud 9' and ready to rock and roll as the LORD directs or so I thought.

The funding of the ministry ended so the LORD and I were in constant conversation!

The temporary housing option was concluding in a week and I did not have a place to go.


## Hosting Home


The LORD prompted me to check the details regarding a home He identified.

While praying about ALL of the facts, the LORD prompted me to contact the California office of a Christian Foundation.

California office would not be able to help me in Georgia so they referred me to the Georgia office.

Phone inquiry did not produce a result so I trusted it was not an option. However, the LORD prompted me to meet with the foundation staff 'in person' and inquire about the options for a hosting home to bring discipleship leaders together from around the world.

The LORD prompted me to inquire about the procedures to follow when the request is from a small ministry which is not operating as a church but, it was the plan of the LORD for me to meet 'in person' with the staff for small ministry funding. I was still 'without a car' in Georgia. Prayers resulted in a special witness driving me to the foundation office and attending as my witness.

The foundation shared details about a church they were funding in Macon. They felt since the church was already being funded it would be easier for me to come in as part of that church and request funding based upon the fact the church was already being funded.

Since I am not part of a church and the funding request is not to be limited to one church, I declined that option.

However, within days it appeared the foundation contacted the church and made the offer to them for my ministry to be included within their funding.

The upsets caused by this connection resulted in the church questioning my ethics as a woman in ministry, etc., etc., etc.

Result: A very serious conversation with the LORD!

The LORD sent a dear woman of God to Macon and I showed her the home the LORD prompted me to check on and it has some potential due to the fact the family paid taxes on two properties since the purchase date due to their deed number accidentally being added to a second property.

The woman was sure I should do what Ruth Heflin did.

Amazing testimony. Ruth met with the owner and the Realtor.

She assured all involved she would not be qualifying to buy since her father would be paying for the property.

The arrangements were made and once the monthly amount was determined, the LORD provided the payment each month.

The woman trusted I should tell the owner and the Realtor the same thing Ruth told her Realtor and the owner of the property.

The problem with this process is my LORD did not tell me I was supposed to promise paying for the property. He told me to point out the error regarding the taxes. When the owner and the Realtor showed no interest in hearing about the facts the LORD provided, I was not given another instruction regarding contact with the Realtor and the owners only wanted communication to take place with the Realtor.

Ruth Heflin and I serve the same LORD.

Our Father does own the cattle on a thousand hills.

We both proceed upon the plan the LORD set forth.

The LORD did not confirm a step to take or a promise to make to the Realtor or to a lender to proceed and the funds were not provided to proceed.

Until the LORD prompts the next action step, there is nothing else to do.

## Chapter 6     Vision About Macon and Georgia

It was late at night. The resistance to the constant upsets regarding 'why is this woman in Georgia' … 'she is interfering with our funding with the foundation' … 'she has no place to call home' … 'the LORD is not providing so she should leave' … I had heard enough. I told the LORD I did NOT need this in my life!

The LORD immediately reminded me of all of the truth revealed to me so I would be prepared to be in Georgia at this time but, I still wanted to know, *Why Georgia?*

I was not happy. In fact, without realizing it I was absolutely upset and demanding to know, *What have I done to be sent here?*

Silence. I waited but, no response. So I asked, *Why would You place me in the armpit of Georgia?*

Clearly, it was not a 'pleasant moment' because I actually questioned the authority of the LORD for placing me in Georgia!

The LORD immediately took me into the glory with Him and showed me a vision. I only saw a map of part of the East Coast of America with the white all around us and the map.

### Georgia.

Then, the state of Georgia pulled up from the map as a brown wood state map with a red heart where Macon is located.

He said, *I did not place you in the armpit of Georgia. Macon is the heart of Georgia.*

When He said this, the red letters of the exact same words appeared to the right of the brown map of Georgia exactly as He spoke the words.

The heart did not make a connection with me!

Why? I was still in my upset when I told God, *Nobody is telling me Macon is the heart of Georgia!*

### Nebraska.

The LORD expanded the map of America to include more than the Eastern half of the nation to show me the Nebraska map exactly as he showed the Georgia map. It was a brown map which pulled up and away from the national map.

There was a red heart and He said, *Nebraska is the heart of America* as the red letters of the exact same words appeared to the right of the brown map of Nebraska exactly as He spoke the words to me and provided the scene.

**Vision.**

Sometimes, it's easy to slip back 'into the natural' while the LORD is sharing a major vision 'in the supernatural'.

**California.**

Before I realized what I was doing, I started explaining to the LORD I did not come to Georgia from Nebraska as if the LORD did not realize this fact!

**Training in Nebraska.**

The LORD 'already knowing my thoughts' **(Matthew 9:4, Luke 5:22 and 9:47)** continued to explain His truth in the midst of my concern, *I trained you in Nebraska, the heart of the nation, to be prepared for the assignment in Georgia.*

Everywhere the LORD sent me globally, the farm experience absolutely prepared me for the living conditions I would experience to fulfill upon an assignment within the nations where the LORD directed my path. However, I was quick in my mind to remind the LORD I flew to Georgia from California and I was in California a few decades after Nebraska.

Within the few seconds of my human explanation in my mind, the LORD had already expanded the national map to include California.

**California.**

I looked for the state map of California to rise up from the map but, it did not.

No heart appeared on California.

The region is beautiful when you are viewing it 'in person' but, the overview clearly reveals the region is a desert.

Then, it hit me!

Desert.

Exactly 40 years as a resident in the desert.

Unable to breathe in that moment.

Panic set it!

Serious heart palpitations were evident!

Without thinking about how it would sound to the LORD the words came out of me like a rushing white water river, *Georgia is my promised land?*


**Preparation.**

The LORD let me sit with the words a very, very long moment before He responded.

First, He reminded me of my childhood 'sentence', ***They are really nice people but they just don't get it*** while I was living in Nebraska hearing the conversations from a human perspective of how people are experiencing a lot of problems and illnesses, wondering when the LORD is going to show up and do something. It often seems the same today with prayer 'chains' becoming all about the long and longer list of 'who is sick' among us and creating gossip about why they are sick and who else in their family is sick or was sick, etc.

From an early age I wondered why the people did not align and unite together!

I've not been easy on God!

Then, He showed me the view from His perspective of His word to me when I so upset and He asked me, *Don't you want to do what I want you to do?* and He showed me how I easily responded, *I will do anything you want me to do!*

## Georgia.

The LORD was preparing me and capturing my full attention again in that moment when He said, *Georgia is not your promised land. What I am doing in Georgia is My promise to My people.*

Before I could completely take it in the LORD said, *You asked for this assignment.*

Panic, again.

What?

How did I ask for this assignment?

I have not said anything to the LORD about Georgia!

I've not talked to anyone about wanting to be in Georgia!

## Assignment.

Without speaking out loud the LORD knew my thoughts again and He responded, *You wanted Me to send someone so the people in America so they would learn how to operate in the same level of faith and discernment to flow together as My people do in the other nations I sent you to, so I sent you.*

What? You sent me?

Wow.

All of the training in Nebraska and in all of the nations around the globe. It was all done in preparation for these days in Georgia!

**Clues.**

Pieces of the assignment were being revealed as the weeks passed. The clues were not noticed until this moment.

Grateful the LORD only gives us what He knows we can handle 'a little bit at a time' during each assignment!

Tears flowed as the LORD thanked me for each family blessed since He placed my feet on the soil of Georgia.

**America in Crisis.**

The LORD confirmed my time in Georgia is critical for America because the believers must unite within the body of Christ! An urgency was evident which I had not fully noticed before other than the message about His currency.

The LORD knew all of this before guiding me through the preparation of the books on Faith, Storehouse, and Currency!

Then, the LORD quickly shifted the scene and reminded me of the amazing fellowship and worship in Ghana.

**Ghana, West Africa.**

A significant shift happened when the LORD placed my feet on the soil of Africa. I had often heard once you are in Africa, life will never look the same. The people sharing this statement were absolutely right!

The level of worship, discernment, discipleship, and the flow of love while in fellowship with the believers causes nearly ALL to desire to gather together praising the LORD often, sharing blessings and testimonies!

The LORD reminded me of that experience and my question of Pastor Sam Korankye Ankrah about the deep level of faith expressed by the people, their discernment and their words confirmed evidence of discipleship. Pastor Sam said, *The people have to pay rent of at least $200 per month and they do not earn $200 per month. They know their LORD is their provider and they are grateful to praise the LORD and share their testimonies every day while thanking the LORD for all He is doing in their lives.*

Re-encouraged, again.

Then, the LORD reminded me what He did to arrange for me to be in Africa. It's a stack of amazing testimonies with the trip being arranged in less than three weeks since I denied I could get to Africa within the seven months after the LORD said I would be going as His witness. He arranged everything without a dime touching my hands. Then, He sent me to meet with a Lutheran pastor who was a pastor for more than 45 years at that point.

The pastor just returned from the World Council of Churches.

He found it odd that I 'spoke like Paul and said I represented the I AM'.

I told him we all do who walk in faith with the LORD so I found it odd that he did not think he represented the I AM.

He said a man from India explained we are to start listening as the LORD shares messages by channeling the words to us through what could be considered a large metal tube from heaven.

I told the pastor channeling and mediums are not of God.

He challenged the statement by telling me that only bible scholars can instruct bible studies since they need to understand the bible. This was a surprise since the man was a pastor for more than 45 years.

While I was asking the LORD how to respond, the pastor said his time was up. He had to rush to a meeting away from the church and he left.

Not sure how long I sat in the car in the parking lot while the tears flowed over the bottom lids.

I cried out to the LORD to know why I was supposed to meet with the pastor and the LORD simply reminded me what I told Him when He asked me to write books about what He is doing with and through me, *You said you only have common sense to share with the people so you think all I am showing you is common sense.*

Repentance was required.

We are no different than the mighty people in the bible. The LORD walked with them and the LORD walks with us each day!

92

# Chapter 7    Unity 'For The Sake Of America'

The LORD confirmed why He placed my feet upon the soil in Georgia.

He wants me to share the facts He provided with the believers who are willing to unite together NOW in Georgia and beyond **'For The Sake Of America'**.

His vision continued to show me how His GLORY will spread from Georgia across America like a mighty flood!

Scripture confirms the truth of this vision: **Habakkuk 2:14.** *For the earth will be filled with the knowledge of the glory of the Lord, as the waters cover the sea.*

Wow! He sent me from sea to sea, across the earth of America to share His knowledge and help the people gain His understanding so they will operate with His wisdom, align as His army and do what He is asking of us to do in these days.

Jesus confirmed this truth before He went to the cross.

**John 17:22-23.** *And the glory which You gave Me I have given them, that they may be one just as We are one:*

*23 I in them, and You in Me; that they may be made perfect in one, and that the world may know that You have sent Me, and have loved them as You have loved Me.*

What was required? Pray!

So much resistance to aligning with fellow believers!

Aligning with the LORD's will and uniting together as Christians seems foreign to Americans within denominations while it was the LORD's plan prior to and especially since Jesus came to earth! Our loyalty is to the LORD, it is NOT to a building or a denomination.

As the Body of Christ we do not operate 'as the members of one body' since we are not 'aligned together in unity',**Roman 12.**

As a woman boldly asked me within the past month, *Are you still a Lutheran or will you come to our Methodist church or do you just fellowship here and there and everywhere?*

My answer is easy, *I am a Christian. I fellowship with the believers of the only living LORD.*

Quickly due to wanting specific clarification she asked, *Yes but, what type of Christian are you?*

Tears started to well up in my eyes for I knew she was lost as I answered her. The Holy Spirit tears fell over the lower lids as I responded, *I am a follower of Christ. Is there something I can do to bring truth to you and bless you during your faith walk?*

### How Can I Reach The People In The Region?

The LORD immediately drew my attention to a local Christian TV station. He prompted me to call the manager.

To my surprise, the man immediately answered the phone and he agreed to meet with me the next day for a cup of coffee.

Trusting I needed a driver for an hour, a dear friend agreed to take me to the local coffee shop.

More than four hours later, the meeting was starting to conclude with the station manager laughing about the fact the LORD told him as soon as he heard my voice on the phone that the meeting would take several hours so he should not plan on a brief meeting over a cup of coffee.

We serve an awesome LORD!

### Unity.

Trusting the man realized the depth of the message within the vision and that the LORD has confirmed: *Unity is critical in these days for we are NOT focused upon His plan for the Body of Christ to unite together and proceed as ONE body, a separate and set apart people, a peculiar people, a holy nation filled with*

*Faith and functioning in His Storehouse while operating based upon His currency. Therefore, whatever happens or changes in the world it will not affect the people of the only true living LORD.*

The LORD prompted me to re-confirm the specific details with the TV station manager one more time before we parted.

### Message About Unity In the Region 20 Years Prior

The TV station manager attended a monthly men's fellowship luncheon the next day. He called immediately after the meeting and he sent an email with a word shared during the meeting.

A man entered the luncheon and handed the word to the TV station manager. The man was not known by anyone at the meeting. He had not attended a meeting with the men's fellowship prior to this luncheon. The word he provided was shared with leaders in the region by Graham Cooke at least twenty years prior.

It was the first trip the LORD prompted Graham to make to America and the LORD directed him to go to Macon, Georgia!

Our LORD has a tremendous sense of humor!

The word by Graham with several Christian leaders in the region was clearly focused upon unity.

Due to the length of **Graham Cooke** word, I'm only sharing one part. *We believe that GOD is saying to you that we all need to work together in such a way because "where the brethren dwell together in unity I will command blessing. And I want to be so* *close in your friendships that I will plant my feet in the very midst of you and what you become in your friendships your churches will become in their own unity." That is a very important thing because I believe God is asking you to dismantle the powers that are over this area to work toward seeing a clear heaven emerge. The devil is the prince of the power of the air and he lives in the atmosphere. As you dismantle the powers, you see it is unity in CHRIST that unhinges the enemy - always that unity. You can't have spiritual warfare while you are killing each other off. We can't have spiritual warfare while you are jealous of each (other) or while you are withholding things from each other. Where the brothers dwell together in unity, there GOD commands blessing and unity and unhinges the enemy. That is why the enemy is doing everything he can to keep us from being one.*

### Inspired To Share The Vision And The Word!

This is the confirmation I was looking for to re-connect with the pastors and leaders within the region to share the vision the LORD showed me and to provide a copy of the word from Graham Cooke.

### Challenges.

The majority of people only wanted to hear a few details over the phone.

The few who did meet with me declared the LORD would not have shown such a vision to me specifically about Macon and they were aware of the word from Graham Cooke as they either attended the meeting with Graham, they saw the word shared among the leadership in the region or they heard about it from a pastor or prophet who attended the meeting when Graham was in Macon.

At first, I felt defeated. But, that is the liar 'at work'.

Then, within a week, the LORD prompted me to view the news feed on Facebook. This is not a typical part of my day but, it was an amazing part of this day!

The post was from one of the pastors I met with, a man who said the LORD would not have shown me the vision about the state map with a heart on the map where Macon is located. He shared the exact photo with his children pointing to the map and words.

It was another year before the LORD directed my path to find this mural within what is known as the 'old Macon mall'. The store is gone and the mural covers the area which used to be the entire glass door entrance to a major store.

Amazing how we are with each other when we are ALL claiming to be joint heirs if we truly are with Christ.

In fact, the Holy, Holy, Holy song I inserted is the exact song we sang in the Lutheran Church. The words are identical in the version I inserted and yet, they were provided by the United Methodist Church as an insert of a song which is part of their hymnal.

Christ did not train up disciples to make some Lutheran, some Methodist, some Presbyterian, and some Baptist. We are to be one body with many members!

Since Christ is in the midst when two or more gather, imagine what we could do if we would unite together as one body of Christ!

It was not several churches in Corinth, it was the Corinthians.

It was not several churches in Phillip, it was the Philippians.

Christ did not send out disciples to do anything beyond spread the Gospel so all who have ears to hear would know the same truth throughout the region: Christ is the LORD of LORDs, KING of KINGs.

He and the Father are one and Christ gave us the glory that we might be one as He and the Father are one, **John 17:22.**

## Chapter 8     Don't Be A Nimrod

Within a few weeks, the LORD arranged for me to move to a special temporary location with a widow.

His timing was impeccable. Her son was in the final days of his challenges due to ALS, Lou Gehrig's disease and yet, she was filled with peace within the first few days of my visit before he passed away. His funeral was at the end of my first week with her.

Within three days, her oldest daughter and the 'connecting sibling' for family gatherings, a strong core for her family was dealing with challenges due to viral spinal meningitis. She lost all memory and the ability to function in her life and in her home. She did not remember that brother had passed away or who her husband was, etc.

Tough days and yet my hostess was filled with peace to deal with all of the hospital visits and the facts which her daughter was not able to comprehend during the second week of my visit.

## Don't Be A Nimrod

Just when I started to feel relaxed in a peaceful environment, trusting I was in the right temporary location and doing all the LORD was asking, hopeful that I was aligned with God's will and His plan for these days I thought I heard Him tell me, ***Don't be a Nimrod.***

Shocked. I sat, silent. Then, I know I heard Him tell me once again, ***Don't be a Nimrod.***

This was disturbing.

This status required a lot more prayer!

## Another Book?

***LORD you are telling me to not be a Nimrod and prepare another book at the same time. This is confusing!***

The LORD was silent. I continued to pray.

He comforted me and I rested.

## Prayer

Without realizing it, I went to the people to ask them what they want in another book!

Everybody confirmed the same request. They wanted a book on prayer.

Everywhere I travel, I am asked to email and text the prayers I pray while in fellowship with believers. So, this made sense.

Clearly, it's not 'easy' to reconstruct the prayer 'after the fact' because the LORD is with me during the prayer time and He helps me identify the exact needs and words 'in the moment' while I am praying with the people for their exact situations or praying with them on behalf of issues their friends and family are facing.

Finally, after so many requests, I agreed to prepare a prayer pamphlet.

Well, the LORD had other plans!

The prayer pamphlet resulted in the prayer chapter becoming Chapter 10 within the next book: *A Wake Up Call: It's Restoration Time!*

How did this happen? Once the chapter on prayer was taking shape, the LORD prompted me to add a chapter before the prayer chapter on relationship with Him since it is important to be in relationship with Him to pray deeply with Him. As He kept adding a topic and another topic, the prayer pamphlet was absolutely turning into a book.

I stopped. Why? I trusted this was not the plan.

I prayed.

I thought I heard the LORD say, ***Don't be a Nimrod*** again.

This seemed very odd as I trusted the LORD would not be calling me a Nimrod.

A yikes moment for sure.

While continuing to pray, I thought I heard the LORD say the same words a little louder, *Don't be a Nimrod.*

Now, I was getting concerned. My thought: *Was the LORD not pleased with the content of the book so far?*

So concerned I did not speak it out loud for I do know our words have power!

Silence.

The LORD was silent so long, I finally asked the question I was not sure I wanted an answer to, *LORD are you calling me a Nimrod?*

The LORD merely responded, *Research Nimrod and tell My people why they do not want to be a Nimrod.*

I did not know about the exact meaning of the name Nimrod but, I did know the name and the phrase meant it was not good.


## Mystery of Noah's Great-Grandson Revealed
## Nimrod, Son of Cush; Son of Ham, Son of Noah


Have you ever heard this saying, *Don't be a Nimrod?*

This is a saying passed generation to generation without attaching the meaning.

Nimrod was the name of the man and it is the definition of the word now since the man rebelled against the LORD.

This is why and how the **_Don't be a Nimrod_** phrase was established.

This was all new news to me.

There are two meanings or definitions for the name Nimrod:

1. mighty hunter, a name he was given early in his life;

2. inept person.

The second definition of the name is the one we hear about to this day.

The reason was not known until the LORD provided the details.

He was capable but, Nimrod rebelled against God.

He was considered mighty.

His land included Babel and other cities.

He is credited for building Nineveh and surrounding cities.

He led the people to build the tower of Babel.

He  was the founder of Babylon.

## How Did Nimrod Gain A Reputation
## Passed On From Generation To Generation?

He gained a reputation for being rebellious toward the LORD.

Nimrod is credited with being the originator of sun worship. He actually declared to the people he had ascended to the sun and upon his return to earth he was to be called Baal, the sun god.

This caused the people under his rule to believe he was the sun god, Baal.

He even established a counterfeit holy day, Sunday.

He did all of this to have people honor him as the sun god, Baal and worship him on the day honoring the sun, Sunday.

Sad but true, as the body of Christ we have participated in this pagan practice every week when we gather and worship together on Sunday. It is not our day of Sabbath, the day set aside each week to rest with and in the LORD.

**Sabbath:** The LORD rested on the seventh day, the Sabbath day, as our example which we are to do every seventh day. Preparing on Friday before sunset and resting 'in the LORD' until after sunset on Saturday.

### What Does Baal Worship Have To Do With Us As Christians?

Silly me, I told the LORD Baal worship was ancient worship.

Without a moment's hesitation the LORD confirmed, *Baal worship is current.*

While sitting in front of my computer shocked to hear the news about Baal being current worship, the LORD prompted me to *Google the names for Baal.*

To my complete surprise, the names are the same and also identified in capitals: God, Lord and Master of the universe.

Not sure how long I stared at the screen.

Even though I did not realize the full impact at the time, tears flowed while I sat and stared.

## Chapter 9    Baal Worship

### Worship of Baal was Comfortable and It Continued

The flood, the ark, our second chance to 'get it right' was already headed in the wrong direction!

This status being repeated generation after generation is exactly what has kept the people who believe in the only living LORD bound through pagan worship, rituals, festivals and traditions, including Sunday gatherings, with Christmas and Easter holidays established to worship other gods and not the only true living LORD. The holidays we celebrate are not based upon the truth.

What we are doing by participating with the pagans is not Christian. We reverted to 'doing as the Gentiles do' which is wrong.

The LORD was revealing a lot more than what He wanted me to insert into a book about prayer, relationship and restoration!

## Christ Gave Us The Truth

Gave it my best shot by reminding the LORD the truth was provided after Nimrod was dead when our Christ came to Earth.

The LORD immediately confirmed the truth was replaced with the same pagan worship within 300 years when Constantine merely inserted Christian facts where He wanted to insert them within the pagan worship calendar.

The Hebrew calendar which confirms the truth about our Jewish feasts and festivals was replaced with lies by Constantine.

## Constantine Re-Confirmed Pagan Worship
## It was Comfortable, Known to Him
## Through His Leadership, Constantine Ordered It
## Baal Worship Continued

The LORD prompted me to research the truth about Constantine since the church has declared he is credited with legalizing Christianity. That is all I knew before the LORD prompted me to do this research.

Pagan worship was continued after Christ was with us and the disciples shared the wisdom and truth region to region.

In 312-325 AD Constantine merged our Hebrew heritage, our Jewish / Christian beliefs and history with his beliefs and pagan worship rituals and dates.

We were grafted in through Christ and therefore we were no longer to operate as the Gentiles. However, Constantine placed us right back into the same position Nimrod established.

Everything about our true history changed.

What we think we know about our history is because we became aligned with pagan worship of other gods when Constantine decreed it and the Council of Nicaea proceeded to structure the 'church' separate from the truth.

We have not questioned it. We have accepted it as the truth.

Therefore, we have continued to worship other gods and we have participated in pagan worship rituals in the same manner for the past two centuries while we have called it Christian.

Many Christians find it difficult to identify their 'idols' today due to the many compromises and the fact we have tolerated instead of taking a firm stand upon the truth and passing the truth from generation to generation.


**Sunday.**

Sunday was not our day of worship.

We prepared on Friday to worship and 'rest in Him' on Sabbath.

Constantine's decree: ***On the venerable day of the Sun let all magistrates and people residing in the cities rest, and let all workshops be closed.***

The decree also stated farmers could continue to work in the fields 'for production of the harvest' and they would not be affected by continuing to work.

The sun god was honored during both the Equinox (Easter/Ishtar fertility ritual vs. Resurrection) and Winter Solstice (Christmastide / Yuletide). The first of the harvest was dedicated to the sun god on these dates.

Some sources say Christians had celebrated on Sunday since The Messiah was born and Constantine was not motivated by a hatred for Jews in changing the traditions as confirmed in Hebrew.

However, Constantine clearly chose pagan worship and changed the dates, merging the details of true believers with the rituals and traditions of pagans and their worship. Plus, he spoke against and discredited the Jews while blaming them for killing the Messiah.

**Constantine, Credited with Establishing Christianity**

Many churches, denominations, and non-denominations, honor Constantine with establishing Christianity or 'making it legal'.

However, he was a politician.

He made a series of decrees which controlled the people and the Council of Nicaea. He made a major political move by appeasing Christians with the merger of facts in the bible with pagan dates and worship. Generation to generation, the muddy process continued and we are merged into honoring the pagan rituals. To this day we worship on Sunday and pagan holidays.

As confirmed within the accounts of the Council of Nicaea, Constantine spoke against the Jews and Hebrew traditions when he declared:

*"And truly, in the first place, it seems to everyone a most unworthy thing that we should follow the customs of the Jews ... having stained their hands with a nefarious crime, are justly blinded in their minds. It is fit, therefore, that rejecting the practice of this people, we should perpetuate to all future ages the celebration of this rite, in a more legitimate order, which we have kept from the first day of our "Lord's" passion even to the present times. Let us then have nothing in common with ... the Jews." Council of Nicaea record.*

So, to this day, we celebrate sun god worship to Baal, and all sun gods through the centuries.

We celebrate the birth of Mithra the son of the sun god who became the sun god, and other gods born on December 25.

We join in the worship of 'other gods' when we join in with the Christmastide / Yuletide worship during the pagan advent time of preparation for the honoring of their gods on each Sunday for four weeks prior to and on December 25 each year.

The new calendar established by Constantine and the Council merged the truth about Christ, the son of God, born at the time of the Feast of Tabernacles in mid-October with the birth of the sun god's son, Mithra.

Mithra was the son of Osirius the Egyptian king of the dead, and Isis an Egyptian goddess of magic, fertility, and motherhood.

How was Mithra referred to by the followers? As 'the lamb'.

In fact, he was often depicted in drawings with a lamb being carried on his shoulders. He was to be honored as the son of god and the good shepherd. Followers trusted he was the way, the truth, the light, the life and the word. Ah, the closest counterfeit!

Celebrations were made similar for both the pagans and Christians: baptisms, communion, and Sunday worship which was established to honor the sun god by Constantine's decree.

The following of the sun god's son, Mithra, was considered a cult. In fact, after his death, followers became known as the **Cult of Isis**.

In many accounts of that time frame, they supposedly thrived and their region flourished under each of the future Emperors who continued honoring the sun god.

**Truth will set us free!**

**We can choose align with truth today!**

This year, Hanukkah is actually celebrated from December 25, 2016 to January 1, 2017. We can immediately re-align with the truth, with our true traditions, the feasts and festivals which Christ, the disciples, and the fellowship of the believers followed.

The key festivals and feasts for the remainder of the 2016 to 2017 year 5777 are as follows:

| | | |
|---|---|---|
| Rosh Hashana | Oct 3-4 | The Jewish New Year |
| Yom Kippur | Oct 12 | Day of Atonement |
| Sukkot | Oct 17-23 | Feast of Tabernacles |
| Shmini Atzeret | Oct 24 | Eighth Day of Assembly |
| Simchat Torah | Oct 25 | Day of Celebrating the Torah (First five books of the Bible) |
| Hanukkah | Dec 25-Jan 1 | Festival of Lights |

With the truth 'in hand' I know we can do better.

We are individually responsible.

We are, individually and globally, the Church.

When we are armed with the truth, we can, and I hope we will, proceed in faith and share the truth by doing all we can to help set the captives free!

The current calendar, dates, and events are not based upon the truth. This is why we are not aware of the true Hebrew calendar.

I cried out to the LORD: *I love You! Believers love You!*

He answered, **My word is true. If you love Me, keep My commandments.**

Tears flowed while I quickly scrolled through the list. The main commandments are mentioned often: do not kill, do not commit adultery, do not covet, do not steal, do not take God's name in vain, do not bear false witness, and honor our parents.

There are three key commandments which are not typically emphasized:


**No other gods before Me,** preceded by: **I am the LORD thy God;** I had not noticed the difference in the 'all capital letters' of LORD prior to God's prompting research of the *Names of God*.

**Do not make idols,** including any possession, or any person, or any thing which we give more attention to than our LORD.

**Honor the Sabbath and keep it holy.**


Shocked to the core!

Plan was simple. We did not proceed upon the plan!

Without realizing the truth, while keeping up traditions and not seeking the facts behind the holidays, we have placed other gods before the LORD.

We have made other idols and graven images by proceeding with pagan rituals and holidays.

We have not honored the Sabbath, the 7th day, the day of rest that our LORD established from the beginning of time, a day we are to honor each week, or kept it holy!

God kept the message simple and clear in the bible.

We are experiencing the same faith walk with God today.

God was reminding me that we claim to be His people (fellow believers) while we are not aware of the simple, clear message: The truth as it is confirmed in the bible!

### The Scribes: Which Is the First Commandment of All?

**Mark 12: 28-34.** Then one of the scribes came, and having heard them reasoning together, perceiving that He had answered them well, asked Him, *"Which is the first commandment of all?"*

29 Jesus answered him, "The first of all the commandments *is:* *'Hear, O Israel, the LORD our God, the LORD is one.*

30 *And you shall love the LORD your God with all your heart, with all your soul, with all your mind, and with all your strength.' This is the first commandment.*

31 And the second, like *it, is* this: *'You shall love your neighbor as yourself.' There is no other commandment greater than these."*

32 So the scribe said to Him, *"Well said, Teacher. You have spoken the truth, for there is one God, and there is no other but He.* 33 *And to love Him with all the heart, with all the understanding, with all the soul, and with all the strength, and to love one's neighbor as oneself, is more than all the whole burnt offerings and sacrifices."* 34 Now when Jesus saw that he answered wisely, He said to him, *"You are not far from the kingdom of God."* But after that no one dared question Him.

**Replica of Roman Triumphal Arch of Palmyra, Entrance to Bel/Baal; 2000 year old Structure Destroyed by Isis, 2015; Traveling on to Dubai before going to Palmyra, Syria Unveiled in Front of New York City Hall, September 19, 2016**

People are furious across America. *The Harbinger* author, Jonathan Cahn refers to the arch as another harbinger.

The problem is, we have proceeded with pagan worship which honors the sun god Baal.

As Christians, individually and as a church, we have personally ushered Baal into our worship and our holidays celebrated within our homes, and in the church, across America.

## Chapter 10    Can We Handle The Truth?

**II Chronicles 7:14.** *If My people who are called by My name will humble themselves, and pray and seek My face, and turn from their wicked ways* (REPENT), *then I will hear from heaven, and will forgive their sin and heal their land* (RESTORE).

Is it truly our desire to know the truth and proceed based upon the truth?

What we need to focus upon is healing our land, which is us. We are from the dust of the earth.

We are the LORD's precious 'hunk of dust' which is the land.

Until we are healed, how can our nation be healed?

Once we know the truth, will we align with the LORD's plan for us and for America?

Will we operate within His will or with our own free will?

The choice is ours to make!

Prompted to issue the initial facts to all believers within the body of Christ, especially after hearing people say: *The Lord will do what the LORD wants to do about ...*

**A truth to consider:** We are living in the world and we have compromised with the world.

It is important to remind ourselves that our free will and the world kingdom are separate from the LORD's will and the Kingdom of Heaven.

This is why Jesus taught us to pray: *Thy will be done, Thy Kingdom come on earth as it is in heaven...*

We are the ones the LORD sent.

We are His people who are 'on earth' to align with and do the LORD's will so it will become on earth as it is in heaven.

Due to the depth of the content, I asked the LORD for another confirmation the book *A Wake Up Call: It's Restoration Time* should be released.

The next day I was invited to dinner with a dear couple.

A little background. The LORD introduced me to this couple the first time I was invited to attend a fellowship meeting with a local tent ministry.

That night, the husband told me why I was in Macon before we had ANY conversation.

My initial response: I dismissed the idea! I was leaving soon!

Well, the LORD arranged for the couple to be given a book: ***Binding The Strongman Over America*** by Dr. John Benefiel.

They found the book to be interesting and the LORD told them to loan their copy to me.

He signed the front page and made a list of numbers with the invitation for me to pass it on to the next person, and so on.

Then, I told him about the new book the LORD gave to me, a book which reveals the truth about worship within the church to Baal and the celebration of the pagan rituals and holidays.

**Baal.** The Strongman was identified in the book as Baal.

The book shared with me includes a divorce from Baal decree, Certificate of Marriage to Christ, Writ of Assistance filed by the People of God against Baal, etc. Powerful documents.

However, we have to change our church calendar and stop living as Gentiles.

### Trail of Tears ended in Oklahoma.

The facts in the book are about the 'end of the trail of tears' in Oklahoma, the 3500 year old hieroglyphs found in the caves which are aligned with the sun god worship of Baal.

### Trail of Tears began in Macon, Georgia.

In that moment, the LORD was confirming He placed my feet at the beginning of the trail of tears, in Macon Georgia.

Growing up in the Midwest the process of moving Native Americans on to reservations was a constant conversation.

In California, I witnessed the same 'limited to reservation land and government subsidies' process. However, the depth of what was done when the government structured the move from the East Coast to Oklahoma was absolutely new news to me.

The LORD provided significant evidence of the affect upon the middle-Georgia region when He prompted me to take a friend to the Ocmulgee Mounds in Macon, Georgia.

### Trail of Tears: Native Americans Removed from Macon.

City of Macon and Bibb County are merged into one structure today, a combined City and County government structure happened during elections shortly after I arrived in 2013.

The Bibb County land was taken from the Creek Tribe of Native Americans who were poorly dealt with by the politician:

**William Wyatt Bibb.** Notes from his biography: *Bibb was elected to Congress in 1803 and served four terms. In 1813 he was elected to the U.S. Senate to complete a term of a senator who had resigned and Bibb served until 1816. While in Congress Bibb was an enthusiastic supporter of the <u>efforts to remove the Creek Indians from Georgia and Alabama</u>. He was appointed governor of the Territory of Alabama in 1816 by President James Monroe as a reward for his support of the planter faction that desired Creek lands for large scale cotton cultivation. In 1819 he was elected the first governor of Alabama. He died in office on*

*July 20, 1820 from injuries in a horse-riding accident. Bibb Counties in Georgia and Alabama were named after him.*

Some of the Creek Indians went to court when the first poorly negotiated treaty was thought to be invalid. Bibb found out and arranged a second treaty signing with men who were known to not the leaders of the Tribe.

**Bibb County Alabama.** Named after **William Wyatt Bibb** due to being appointed first Governor of Alabama. Bibb also removed all Creek Indians off their land in Alabama.

The men who were not in the right leadership position to sign the second treaty were later executed by the Creek tribal council for their actions against the people.

The treaties were brought before the court and found to be invalid but the case was not resolved by the court 'in time' for the Creek Native Americans to remain on or return to their land along the east and then the west sides of the Ocmulgee River and beyond.

It was their land as proven in the court but, it was not possible for them to return after the treaties were found to be invalid due to the fact that Bibb arranged deals for the huge cotton plantation(s), settlements and military sites as soon as he arranged for the Creek Indians to be removed. The land taken from the Creek Indians expands far beyond and nearly all of Bibb County Georgia today.

**Tour with an ancestor of the tribe.**

The LORD prompted me to take a woman to the historic site of the Ocmulgee Mounds property without realizing her ancestry includes the Mississippians who inhabited the land which is currently known as the Ocmulgee Mounds and National Monument. The LORD prompted both of us to climb the series of stairs to view the land from the top of the Temple Mound.

# The Native Americans Are a Focus of Repentance Prayers!

**Ocmulgee Burial Mounds**

**Ocmulgee National Monument, Macon, Georgia**

The sky was beautiful with very few light clouds when we arrived. When we were at the top and checking the view in all directions, toward Macon and the museum building on the historic site, the LORD prompted my friend to take photos. He wanted us to see the sky from His perspective.

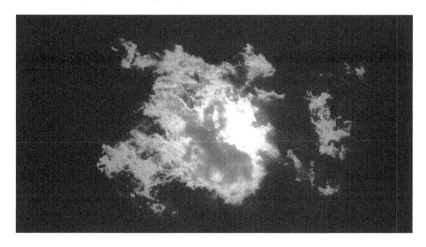

After she took a photo with my camera, she took one with her camera. Then, she took another photo with my camera.

To our amazement, the photos on both cameras were identical!

The LORD was showing us the view from His perspective.

Since the roots in the region have not been dealt with, repented for, full restoration has not taken place and the land has not healed.

*Any man who thinks he can be happy and prosperous*
*by letting the Government take care of him,*
*better take a closer look at the American Indian.*

**Quote by Henry Ford**

## Chapter 11    Baal Activity Evident In America Today

Is the ancient worship of Baal current? *Absolutely yes!*

The LORD confirmed Baal worship is current. 'Knowing my thoughts' the LORD answered my thought about worship of Baal being ancient worship before I asked the question.

### Baal is Speaking to the Orphans

God told me to go to a local orphanage for the sake of a young lady named Lauren.

Since I did not have a car, the LORD sent me to a prayer meeting with a local pastor. He keeps the plan simple!

A house parent from the Masonic orphanage was in attendance. I trusted the was going to provide my ride to the orphanage but, he did not have a car. He would make all of the arrangements for me to meet with Lauren during lunch on Saturday. I just had to find a ride to the orphanage.

Within an hour, God sent two women who were 'cleared' to be at the Masonic home and they agreed to take me on Saturday.

The LORD made all of the arrangements after He prompted me call a pastor for a ride to attend a prayer meeting.

### Orphanage: 11:30 AM, Saturday.

House mother was still asleep.

Lauren invited me into her room.

She showed me a few of her drawings: Satan and Angels.

Everything in her room and conversation was specific.

She said she is ready to go to heaven so God can make her an angel and give her wings. Then, she can go where God needs her to go to help people because she is restricted to her class room and her bed room.

Shocked.

She explained that she is not able to get a second chance from any of the adults here on earth, so in her prayer time she thought she was hearing the LORD's plan for her! Hard to believe!

She was actually listening to the enemy for options to get out of her current situation without realizing it.

She trusted Baal because he said he represented the LORD.

She trusted the queen of heaven since the queen of heaven actually told her that she was Mary, the mother of Jesus Christ.

Instead of the Holy Spirit guiding her, the impostors were instructing her to go to heaven (commit suicide), become an angel and obtain wings. Then, she would to be able to go where she needs to go to heal and help people.

Plus, they told her she could negotiate with God for the fallen angels, the Nephilim, so they could get a second chance because she is not getting a second chance on earth she knows what it is like to not get a second chance from adults. The enemy explained the Nephilim were not given a second chance, either.

As a young girl and even as a college graduate, I did not know anything about Baal, queen of heaven or the Nephilim!

Many have questioned me when this experience is shared because they are not aware of the reference in scripture to the queen of heaven. The LORD had to help me on this once since I'm not a bible scholar. The LORD responded, quickly! *All believers are warned in Jeremiah 44.*

The scripture does warn of the LORD's declaration to any who worship the queen of heaven. During the research of the scripture, the LORD prompted me to check on the definition within the world. The definition states the Roman Catholic Church refers to Mary, the mother of Christ, as the Queen of Heaven.

*LORD we thank You for keeping Your hand upon us while You reveal Your truth to us!*

**Rebellion.** The LORD prompted me to ask Lauren if she was in a bit of rebellion.

Lauren nodded and said, *Yes Ma'am.*

So the LORD prompted me to write the word REBELLION on a napkin in the lunch room and draw a line between the two Ls.

Then the LORD prompted me to explain His truth: *When we are in rebellion we are rebelling against Christ for He the Lion of Judah and that is NOT what we want to be doing as Christians!*

### Prayer.

Lauren requested prayer before I left and that prayer resulted in a new testimony for her in a week and another testimony in two weeks, a testimony related to the fact her life was back on track.

We prayed for the non-believing teacher, for the administrator of the children's home since orphanages are to be called children's homes so they become politically correct in our society.

It is stated by the orphanage employees this change actually helps the children not feel like orphans however, the children are clear about their status. They know they were left at the orphanage and they are not going to their home again. They know they are orphans and therefore, this 'new name' to supposedly be 'politically correct' is a lie.

### Renouncing Prayer.

Powerful all day conference with Rebecca King proceeding through multiple pages of the renouncing prayer of the Masonic oaths. The goal of the Illuminati taking over Masons is to take us back to Egypt, to align worship with the gods and goddesses leading to Isis, the cult of Isis within sun god Baal worship.

NOTE: Reverend Harmon R Taylor, former New York Grand Chaplain, 1983-1984 provides his letter requesting a demit from all bodies of the Masonic fraternity after learning the truth. His letter is available 'on line' for review of the facts.

### Plans of the enemy.

The enemy is working diligently with the youth, and especially the orphans! The structure in all communities established within the Masonic lodge format has affected all towns and cities in America. Gary Kah received significant documents which confirm the truth and they can be found on his ministry web site.

**Masonic home of Georgia is on the highest hill in Macon, "*The heart of Georgia.*"** The LORD asked me to Google the information. His sense of humor is amazing.

The article about the history of the Masonic orphanage confirms 650 acres on the highest hill in the region with 100 acres donated for the home to be built because (in italics, as the LORD showed it to me in the vision and exactly as it appears on the Masonic home web site) *Macon is the heart of Georgia.*

This confirmed the vision the LORD gave me, again, regarding why He sent me to this region.

**Transportation Request.**

That night, I cried out to the LORD for a car so I could go to the school and to the home to meet with the social worker and the administrator. It was midnight. I was going to rest.

At midnight, a woman I had not met heard the LORD tell her, *Donate the car to the woman your parents have told you about for several (9) months, because she needs to go where I need her to go instead of where people are willing to take her.*

Her teenage son's initials are BMW and the car is a 1999 BMW station wagon which he was going to start driving in a few months.

She told her son what the LORD shared with her and she asked him to pray about it.

He returned to talk with her in a few moments.

The LORD told him to release the car to me to go where the LORD needs me to go so I can do what the LORD needs me to do.


**Car provided.** With keys in hand by Thursday morning, I asked the LORD for confirmation, *Should I drive to the school or the Masonic home?* The LORD merely whispered, *I've got this!*

I still asked two more times.

His response was the same each time.


**Testimony.**

The next Sunday, a van from the home brought the children to fellowship. Lauren grabbed the microphone and wanted to give a testimony.

She kept pointing at me, *That woman was told by God to come and see me because I am special to Him.*

Lauren then stated many quotes from our brief meeting, clearing up who Baal and the Queen of Heaven are, who we are as joint heirs with Christ vs. becoming an angel, etc.

### Prayer for her teacher.

Then, she shared a major confirmation of the truth about our LORD, *On Thursday morning my non-believing teacher told me, 'I never give a second chance but, I am supposed to give you a second chance ... I never clear a record but, I am supposed to clear your record ...'*

Everything in her life was turned around by our LORD!

Lauren credited the LORD and shared the brief note about rebellion which I left with her on the napkin in the lunch room.

### Prayer with her mother.

Lauren shared what she learned with her mother, a woman who was dealing with a divorce and unable to care for her daughters due to not having a job.

Her mother took her to her grandmother's home and she could only help with the younger daughter so Lauren confirmed she was dropped off at the home in Macon at the same time the LORD placed my feet on the soil in Macon!

Since Lauren shared the prayers and testimony of what the LORD did in her life with her mom, her mom started praying what

Lauren called 'the new way to pray our prayers' about her own situation and she got a job!

### Car ministry.

The LORD was thanking me for the car ministry while I was saying I can finally go where He needs me to go. The LORD showed me a scrapbook with before and after photos of each of the families who provided rides during the 18 months I was in Macon without a car. The LORD caused tears to flow by showing me His truth because I trusted I was not 'doing all I could do' before the car was provided!

## Will We Pray Believing?
## Will We Humble Ourselves, Seek the LORD
## Turn From Our Wicked Ways and Pray The Truth
## About Our Situations to Hear from Heaven & Heal?

A woman loved hearing the details during an AGLOW meeting in the Athens, Georgia area.

She was fascinated with the orchestration the LORD provides regarding the each of the daily details. However, she found it impossible to consider the LORD would do so much through me and yet, leave me in a temporary status while working for Him.

It did not make sense to her that I am 'temporary in the region' because she trusted serving the LORD means having an amazing home to operate from and spend time with the LORD!

Easy for me to confirm temporary is exactly what is required for me to be available to 'impact a region' for the Kingdom!

The next morning, she said she prayed to know the LORD would do more for her while she traveled and worked for Him. She said she asked the LORD to confirm how she will live and travel with Him while she is doing ministry.

She thought the LORD told her she would be traveling in limos and staying in five star resorts.


*LORD help those who do not know what is required to serve You in these days for the body of Christ is in need of servants who will go where You need them to go, to do what You need them to do, and say what You need them to say, while they continue to stand firm in the midst of the multitude until Your people hear Your truth.*


## High Point Church
## Macon, Georgia


Brother Don became the name recognized long term for Pastor Donald Van Hoozier., High Point Church in Macon, Georgia.

About 17 years before we met 'in person' in Macon, the LORD gave me a word to share with Brother Don.

It was a private word for him so when he took my hand due to recognizing my voice (perhaps it was because I was the only one without a Southern accent attending a day filled with multiple baptisms) and asked me about the word the LORD shared with him through me years before, the only fact the LORD shared was *You were warned because you passed the baton too early*.

Brother Don shed a few tears because a younger pastor was brought in to expand the church and develop a youth group. Instead of expanding the church, he wanted to take over and change everything about the services. His actions actually caused such a significant split in the church it was difficult to recover.

Brother Don was well known among the American and global prophets and most shared the pulpit at High Point Church. Sometimes Bob Jones and John Paul Jackson or Arthur Burt (Wales) would share the pulpit together on the same Sunday.

Brother Don wanted to know if I had any family in Macon. I confirmed I did not have family in Georgia. I was only remaining in the region for an assignment the LORD was sharing one step at a time. Brother Don then prayed a powerful confirming prayer about the commitment required for a servant to proceed only upon what the LORD shares moment by moment.

After the baptism, I was invited to tour the house next door.

## Childhood Home of John Birch

The house was being remodeled and converted into the offices for the church, a newer kitchen, a conference room, and a sitting area. It was a unique design. When I asked about the original structure of the building, I was informed it was the home of the Birch family, the childhood home of John Birch.

The LORD reminded me of the details regarding the John Birch Society which were shared with me within months of the flight to Georgia.

The John Birch Society was frowned upon since it was considered to be a group operating against the government of America. The leaders met with Christians across the country to inform them of the truth about the Federal Reserve, the IRS, and actions taken which affected the original structure of America as a Republic. The Society was maligned perhaps due to being misunderstood. Members were considered to be pursuers of conspiracy theories against the United States government. The Birch family knew the truth which John shared during his time serving in Intelligence while he was a Captain in the United States Air Force serving in China during WWII.

The truth is the members of the John Birch Society were sharing deep truth hidden from Americans about the take over of the currency and banking structure in America. The Society knew the Federal Reserve and the IRS were not government entities and the two entities were going to destroy the economy of America.

Both entities were formed during meetings in Georgia.

The Society met with and asked the family of John Birch to borrow his name for the Society since John served in WWII and knew the Communist / Chinese plans for the future.

John was hearing the 'bigger picture' of the future plans for America after the actions taken in Georgia with the establishment of the non-government entities of the Federal Reserve and the IRS.

Then, the turn-over of all gold to the Federal Reserve with only fiat currency used prior to the war, and the establishment of a social welfare structure called the Social Security system which would collect from employers and employees and be presented as a pension structure that employers and citizens would fund to supposedly benefit citizens upon retirement.

All of this was structured in Georgia.

China knew their part 'in the future structure' by then. The United States was already supplying war materials to China while sanctioning Japan. Japan's anger resulted in the attack on Pearl Harbor. More facts about the 'behind the scenes' actions by the government are included within Chapter 20.

No matter who John shared the truth with in America, as an intelligence officer or as a concerned citizen, the truth was evidently shared with leaders in China and this is what supposedly caused John to be shot in the back and buried in China.

Due to John's work in China and his knowledge of what was going on in China, the leaders of the John Birch Society established the organization shortly after WWII and named the Society in John's honor with permission from his family.

Since I've not been a member of the John Birch Society, these are a few facts I knew due to a video friends shared a few months prior to my flight to Georgia in 2013. More facts were provided when I researched topics by the LORD's prompting after I was 'boots on ground' in Georgia.

The LORD was dove-tailing so many details together it was amazing to realize the divine orchestration.

All of the details shared while I was visiting High Point Church on that specific Sunday became beneficial within a few days!

So many 'introductions over time' which meant something now.

So many 'meetings during prior years' providing facts which would bring it all together in these days through people I had not met prior to God's three week plan for me to be in Georgia.

We serve an awesome God!

## The LORD Is Sending A Bulldozer
## The Plans Of Man Will Not Succeed
## This Vision Appeared to Producers With Daystar TV
## Vision Interpreted by John Paul Jackson

The producers with Daystar TV received a vision.

John Paul Jackson interpreted the vision while being interviewed by Joni Lamb.

Joni shared the brief facts of the vision: The producers were watching a video feed. They were waiting for the exact moment when they needed to insert the story.

Within moments, the equipment appeared to malfunction.

This happened in 2012, before the election.

The LORD confirmed He was sending a bulldozer.

He showed the bulldozer going through the white house.

John Paul Jackson gave an accurate interpretation before the 2012 election regarding what would be unfolding before the next election. The LORD was confirming more would unfold before the bulldozer would appear.

The LORD prompted me to search for the vision details within You Tube. It is available for viewing by inserting the key details.

Now, in 2016, we are watching the bulldozer experience.

More truth is  being revealed to the people in these days about the 'behind the scenes' actions than at any time in our history.

Christians are waking up from coast to coast.

Grateful!

## Chapter 12    A Wedding Word: 'For The Sake Of America'

A special wedding was scheduled.

The couple became special to me the first night we met.

They were prompted to speak into my life.

The groom had a prophetic word about my life and why I was in the region. The bride was given a specific scripture which confirmed the word. It was a significant blessing!

The memories they created in that moment will definitely be added to the amazing memories being created during the gathering with friends for their wedding.

The special moments created with me happened prior to their amazing engagement day, a day when the groom walked in a circle pattern for quite a while before he focused upon his bride and asked her to marry him.

When I entered the room, I took a seat at the far end of the row. Within moments I heard the LORD say, *Move up two rows.*

While I was busy explaining to the LORD I am not part of the immediate family and I trust the empty rows are saved for the family the LORD gently asked, *Please move up two rows.*

As soon as I moved to my new seat at the far end of the row, a couple entered the room and immediately sat next to me.

The wife and I kept busy taking casual photos before the wedding. In a few moments, the husband leaned toward us and told me: *We need to talk after the ceremony.*

His words remained in my mind during the entire ceremony.

While the photos were being taken of the bridal party, the man started talking to me about Macon and the vision given to Bob Jones *For The Sake Of America.* Bob Jones was very close to the couple and he passed the details on to them since He was dealing with health issues.

Excited because it felt like the LORD sent a couple to come alongside and help. But each time I started to tell him what the LORD was revealing to me about Macon and Georgia, the man said, *The LORD already told me.*

Finally, I stopped and told him how much I appreciated the fact the LORD brought us together for His plan and purpose.

However, the man was very quick and clear to confirm they would not be moving to Macon or doing anything about the vision. They are heavily involved in another ministry which takes up all of their time.

**Vision.** The man revealed the LORD is preparing the region between Macon, Georgia and Moravian Falls, North Carolina *For The Sake Of America.*

**Macon.** The LORD placed me in Macon. While I shared details about the assignment with people I thought could be trusted, the LORD revealed the many times He had people remind me of the three days of **Jonah in the Whale** during the days when I felt unqualified to go where He needed me to go, to do what He needed me to do.

Now the LORD was reminding me how I thought I knew the book of Jonah but, I was not aware of the shift in the assignment revealed in Chapter 4 of Jonah!

The LORD re-focused Jonah so he could gain the LORD's perspective about Nineveh, where 120,000 'in the city did not know their left from their right'.

The LORD was prompting me to research the statistics and it appears the Macon population is at the 120,000 level.

Plus, Macon is 'in trouble' as a top ten crime city in America!

**Moravian Falls.** The LORD sent me to Moravian Falls and Prayer Mountain. The power realized while on Prayer Mountain praying for friends was evident before the testimonies were provided. Powerful testimonies from people who had no idea they were being prayed for while the LORD arranged for me to be on Prayer Mountain Wednesday evening, January 28, 2015.

**Example:** A friend was not able to smoke a cigarette after smoking since the age of 13. At the same time we were praying, she tried three cigarettes and did not like the taste. She has not smoked a cigarette since that night.

### Feeling Alone And Pregnant

Have you every felt so full of what the LORD reveals that you feel pregnant and ready to share the excitement with family?

Well, that is what happened because I moved up two rows!

Immediately, I left the reception.

I called the couple I met the first night I attended the tent ministry because the LORD prompted me to remember the truth revealed by the husband since he knew why the LORD placed me in Macon before we shared a conversation.

They were available and fixing dinner.

Everything the LORD revealed up to this point was 'in preparation' of receiving the vision in this moment and hearing the man confirm it was being released to me 'on purpose'.

After receiving the John Paul Jackson and Arthur Burt confirmations of this word and vision, I felt honored. The LORD was bringing it all together now so it could be fulfilled upon.

The details filled the next couple of hours of fellowship.

My concern: *How Can I Wake Up The People in Georgia if Religion is the focus vs. being a Christian?*

The LORD had already confirmed the total number of fellowships, churches, and gatherings of people who were believers in Macon was more than twice the number quoted by people in the local churches.

The LORD provided significant evidence of the church structures causing people to depart from the fellowship and create new fellowships and gatherings.

Over time, the religious spirit over Macon has become so significant, it was making it nearly impossible for the people to flow together as one body.

## Will We Align With The LORD?

## Will We Follow His Commandments?

The Ten Commandments from our LORD as confirmed by Christ are clear and they provide the brief outline for us as a standard: *Thou shalt have no other gods before me.*

When I shared the truth about honoring the Sabbath, the seventh day and keeping it holy, I was told frequently that the *Sabbath is a Jewish thing.*

Even when I shared the truth, it is one of the commandments, I was told frequently *It was part of the old covenant and we are under the new covenant.* When I stated Christ confirmed the covenant it caused even more upsets!

Shocked.

I asked the LORD what to tell the people questioning the Sabbath as a Jewish thing. The LORD quickly reminded me, *We are a Jewish thing for we are grafted in the moment we claim our salvation in Christ, the Messiah.*

This is the truth and therefore, we are no longer Gentiles and we are not to do as the Gentiles do since it is not who we are as members of the body of Christ with his name in Hebrew being Yeshua Hamashiach.

The LORD was proving to me that the people have become religious in their ways for Christ was clear in what the people call the new covenant when He confirmed in **John 14:15.**

*If you love Me, keep My commandments.*

144

## Quote About Ten Commandments

*I have wondered at times what the Ten Commandments would have looked like if Moses had to run them through the US Congress.*

## President Ronald Reagan

The battle about whether to honor the Sabbath or not is clearly between each of us and the LORD for it is one of His commandments. It has been such a tough challenge, I really felt I was failing the LORD on this assignment.

Instead of wrapping me in His arms and comforting me about my concerns He merely said, *Write about unity.*

I laughed. Nobody wanted to hear about unity, not even the TV station manager or the leadership in the region more than 20 years after the LORD sent Graham Cooke to present the word on unity to Macon. Therefore, I had no reason to write it down for me to read.

However, He said, *Write the unity book.*

Shocked when I heard my response, *A book on unity? What would I use for a cover photo to express unity since the people who say they are members of the body do NOT want to unite on anything!*

Within moments, the LORD provided an amazing photo.

Then, I wanted to know about the title and before I even asked Him the title was provided: *In One Accord.*

I did not have much more to say about the matter.

I was just about ready to ask what the LORD wanted me to write since I had no words let alone a book worth of words when He said, *Good. Unity is My heart. Use My words.*

Long story short, the LORD arranged the scriptures which provide His plan for His people to unite together *In One Accord.*

With about ninety percent of the content written, I was not feeling it was ready to send for editing.

### Are Our Religious Ways, Christian?

Many pastors wanted to meet and hear the details.

Each one wanted me to share the details with their fellowship if I was willing to be fully involved with their fellowship and do everything through their fellowship.

Unity means gathering many fellowships together until the body of Christ is united as one body.

No pastors were willing to support me in uniting the various fellowships and bringing the believers together.

### Will We Change From Our Wicked Ways?

**II Chronicles 7:14.** *If My people who are called by My name will humble themselves, and pray and seek My face, and turn* *from their wicked ways* **(REPENT)**, *then I will hear from heaven, and will forgive their sin and heal their land* **(RESTORE).**

## Do We Need To Gain A New Perspective?

In the depth of my prayers, the LORD said it was important for me to prepare tomorrow, Thursday, because He is sending me to the mountain top on Friday.

On Friday, I asked about timing of departure since I was not clear and I did not have an address to put into the GPS since He did not reveal where I was going beyond saying the mountain top.

The only clue shared Friday morning: ***The LORD wanted me to wait for a call from a pastor until 2:30 since the pastor wanted to meet for lunch that week.***

At 2:30, I drove to the freeway entrance ramp to travel north and that is how the next phase of my journey began.

## Gaining A Mountaintop Perspective

An invitation to be a caretaker was offered in the northeast region of Georgia. However, no specifics were provided beyond the name of the dog I would be taking care of while the owner was working in a different part of the state.

Since everything was so vague, I called a friend living in Woodstock, north of Atlanta. She offered a guest room for the weekend while details were sorted out. I was deeply grateful. Her address was inserted into the GPS and I was on my way north.

Macon is in top ten crime cities in America.

Woodstock (suburb of Atlanta) is in top 25 safest cities!

Immediately, the LORD shared a brief word with me. *You can visit your friend but I have arranged for you to go to the mountaintop.*

Silence.

The moment the car was above the 475 and 75 merge, the sky seemed bluer and it seemed like I could breathe deeper.

When I asked the LORD what was happening, He provided a perspective of what I just lived through while I was in middle-Georgia.

Wow. I felt the physical and emotional twisting and turning in that moment as I did while trying to share the truth, the prophetic words and visions. It was the same while helping all of the people the LORD placed in my path because I was not able to break through the heaviness of the religious spirit which covers the region.

The LORD was taking me to the mountaintop to help me gain a new perspective from His viewpoint above the heaviness over Macon, above the religious spirit which encases the region.

He confirmed it was not going to be possible to break through from underneath. I needed to be beyond it to view the status of Macon from a new perspective.

Even though the details were vague, it was clear this step was part of the LORD's plan for me to go to the mountaintop. I placed the call and declined the offer to stay in the guest room.

Deep in thought, I continued to journey north to the mountain region.

### The Mountaintop Is Real

Two days after my arrival, the teenage daughter of my host offered to show me the walking path she enjoys with her older sister. By the time we reached the half way point, she merely stated the two sisters often stop and relax a moment before returning home.

When I realized what we were viewing, she laughed. She said, *Since you said God was sending you to the mountaintop I thought you would like to know you are physically on the mountaintop and it would be good for you to see the view from the mountaintop.*

She was right. It was a breathtaking 360 degree view.

### Believers Say They Are United In The Region

Grateful to be invited to a church called 'Revive' and a fellowship called 'united believers'. Hopeful.

Weekly meetings of the 'united believers' fellowship are held during the lunch hour on Wednesday.

The meetings were established ten years before I arrived. The people represent different churches and fellowships in the region and since the meetings were held in a different church each month the group is recognized throughout the region.

However, I was not seeing people being added to this group from the different church location they met in each month.

Introduced to a home fellowship known as 'Open Fellowship' while the attendance was minimal and often included only as many as three or four of the same guests each week.

Within a couple of months, the local fellowships I was introduced to started to participate with me during Rebecca King's weekly bible study and conferences.

The people also attended meetings with Prophet Nancy Haney from Alaska, meetings which I arranged in their region when Nancy was traveling in their region. Nancy had plowed the ground for about seven years before the LORD sent me to Georgia. I was hopeful that the meetings would flourish with the additional connections of local leaders to key people in the body of Christ.

After the meetings were arranged, unity was not evident in the region.

When I cried out to the LORD, He arranged for me to return to Macon for the next phase of the journey.

Trusting it was only going to be a few more days since the fulfillment of the vision, the LORD's promise *For The Sake Of America* was not coming to pass while I am remaining in the region.

However, that was a year ago and the LORD has orchestrated even more introductions and he has revealed far more due to my obedience in being where He needs me to be so I can do what He needs me to do and say what He needs me to say.

## Chapter 13    What Will It Take To Unite Believers?

### Living 'In One Accord'

Not 'feeling it' LORD!

Not sure what You can do with the people LORD but, I'm feeling stuck!

### Restoration vs. Revival

The LORD reminded me: *It is the same issue about unity in Georgia as it is in each state across America.*

Since the word was already shared with me, *What the LORD does in Georgia will flood across the nation* the LORD re-focused my attention to the truth He provided when He sent me *In Search of Wigglesworth.*

Sharing a few of the facts the LORD has provided, facts I shared with the people in the region and within *It's A Faith Walk!*

Crying out for revival has not yet produced the results. Why? The body of Christ is in dire need of restoration!

Individually, we are broken. Hearts are damaged. Dis-eases are a constant conversation among believers.

Prayer chains actually end up declaring the work of the enemy in the life of a church member and then, in members of their family.

The LORD has shown me the specifics many times within His word during a mighty journey orchestrated when He sent me *In Search of Wigglesworth*

He gave me a powerful view of the body of Christ in a vision He provided about **Restoration vs. Revival.**

The LORD's bottom line: *If Christ is in the heart, why would the hearts of the people have flat-lined? Why would Christians require being revived?*

During the preparation of *It's A Faith Walk!* the LORD prompted me to insert specific quotes. Due to constant requests for revival, I was shocked to hear the quote by Kathryn Kuhlman within a You Tube video from the meetings at Oral Roberts University in 1974: *It's not Revival, It's Restoration!*

Since *It's Restoration*, all of our focus needs to be upon the process of being restored as a person, as the body of Christ, and as the people who seek restoration of our nation!

**II Chronicles 7:14.** *If My people who are called by My name will humble themselves, and pray and seek My face, and turn from their wicked ways* (REPENT), *then I will hear from heaven, and will forgive their sin and heal their land* (RESTORE).

After sending me *In Search of Wigglesworth*, the LORD prompted me to research the scriptures on revival and on restoration. His word is clear, it's all about restoration!

A few examples:

**Deuteronomy 30:3-13** restoration of all that was lost;

**Psalms 80.** Prayer for Israel's Restoration;

**Psalms 147:3.** He heals the broken hearted.

**Job 33:26.** ... for He restores;

**Job 42.** Job's repentance and restoration;

**Lamentations 5.** Prayer for Restoration;

**Joel 2:25.** He will restore the years;

**Corinthians 4:13.** ... at once the woman was restored to health

Many scriptures on restoration of marriage and family, also.

The LORD restored the temple.

Christ declared the truth when He said the temple would be rebuilt in three days. In three days, <u>He was restored with resurrection power and that same power resides within us</u>!

**Regarding revival:** when I confirm it's all about restoration, people have repeatedly quoted **Psalms 85:6.** *Will You not revive us again, that Your people might rejoice in You?*

However, they are taking the verse out of context by completely bypassing the prior verses: **Psalms 85:4-5.** *Restore us, O God of our salvation, and cause Your anger toward us to cease.*

Yes. There are references to revive in the bible. The people were in the desert. People need to be revived with water when they return from their journey. Plants and animals are also revived with water.

*LORD help us to repent for all actions not aligned with Your will and gain full restoration of our heart and soul for Your word confirms we prosper as our soul prospers. Help us to gather together as a fellowship of believers who are willing to repent, seek You and turn from our wicked ways so You will hear from heaven, heal us and heal our nation!*

A brief excerpt from the portion about the vision within:

*In Search of Wigglesworth*

## The LORD's Vision About Revival

While I was expressing my upset after realizing the people do not remember all the LORD had done in the region, and in the Hebrides and Azusa Street at the same time, I was immediately surrounded by His glory, standing with Him in a very light and bright place.

Lots of lights were shining bright.

It took a moment to realize I was in a hospital, just inside the Emergency room entrance. This provided a view of all the activity coming in from the world.

When the Emergency room doors opened, ambulances were backed up at the entrance with their back doors wide open.

Each ambulance carried what appeared to be an identical 'little white wood church'. Each church was on a gurney. Doctors were confirming the status: ***Dead On Arrival,***since each church had flat lined.

Each one of the emergency staff waited for a different doctor or a team of doctors to show up, to 'revive the church/patient'.

Workers were everywhere, waiting on the expert team. However, before the 'blue cart' team could get to the gurney more and more ambulances were arriving. The ambulances could not get near the emergency room doors since additional ambulances were already lined up at the entrance. As each paramedic opened the back doors of the ambulance, it was clear they were delivering another church to be revived.

In that moment (I have no idea how long I observed this status) the LORD confirmed:

*"This is the condition of My people, My church. This is why I sent you to search for Wigglesworth. The heart is where Christ resides. The Holy Spirit guides in truth, strengthening where and when the people are weak."*

I was stunned, speechless. Wow.

The visual was effective.

This is the condition of our church, today.

This is how the church appears to God, with the health of the church in jeopardy.

Then, I cried out to God: *Lord, what will it take to remind the people about a region known as Sunderland, England, and help them remember how the people were touched while You sent an illiterate man, Wigglesworth, around the world?*

God revealed the sad status of the body of Christ.

It hit my heart like a ton of bricks!

God's confirmations were tearful as I was hearing the truth from the people which matched the words upon God's heart: *"The people do not remember."*

At the time of the vision, I had no idea God was actually tapping me on the shoulder to share the truth about *Restoration vs. Revival* with the body of Christ.

**Bottom line:** *God's plan does not require reviving our 'flat lined' heart! We have life in Christ and He resides in our heart!*

### People From Afar Bring Revival to a Region

This is a consistent request as I travel region to region. The leaders want me to bring revival to their region and revive their fellowship. The LORD often sends me to re-encourage a pastor but, that is different. As a body of Christ we have established a church according to a world structure.

We have not established the church as defined in **Ephesians 2:20**, upon the apostles and prophets with Christ as the Chief Cornerstone. We put all of the responsibility and accountability for the entire five-fold ministry upon the pastor! Even prayer and bible knowledge. Shame on us!!!

This status can and must be turned around. We are each responsible and we are each going to be held accountable!

Repeatedly, people think since God sent me that I was sent to bring revival to their region. However, even though I may not be sent to a region for a long period of time I am sent to share the truth so the people will gather together in one accord and restore each other.

Instead of crying out for revival, for God to do more, may we focus upon restoring each other when we gather together and fellowship with believers as Christ confirmed: **Matthew 18:20.** *"For where two or three are gathered together in My name, I am there in the midst of them."*

God does not send me to 'fix' or 'repair'. He does not send me to a region for a temporary process to be the result whether I am there for a few days or a few weeks.

Everything God tells me to impart to the people is done to activate or reactivate the people, especially those who have become discouraged over time: pastors, teachers, prophets and apostles He has commissioned, and evangelists plus the leaders among the body of Christ.

He provides the instructions regarding everything required to disciple, equip, and train them so they can stand firm in the truth and in faith, to inspire, encourage and disciple others. I often describe what I do as an injection vs. an intravenous feed (drip) aka, giving the people a word at a time.

### Denying Truth

A dear woman of God loved the *In Search Of Wigglesworth* book but, she was sure the details about Wigglesworth learning to read from "Polly" were wrong because her name was not "Polly."

She sent a message through the contact form on my web site since she toured the region in England. She took a photo of the tombstone for Wigglesworth. It also named Wigglesworth's wife.

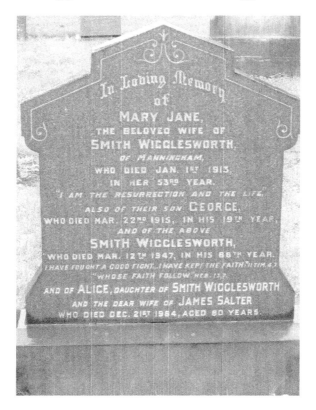

The LORD told me about Wigglesworth's wife teaching him to read the bible and letting him go nation to nation before phones, cars, and planes.

Personally, I was sure the LORD said her name was Polly so that is what I inserted into the book.

Immediately, I took the 'upset' of the woman to the LORD. He told me to Google "Polly" exactly as He said to research Baal.

There it was in print on the page.

Wikipedia stated Polly Featherstone married Wigglesworth.

Wikipedia also confirmed Polly taught Wigglesworth how to read and he only read the bible. The statement about his life also confirmed he did not allow a newspaper in his home, the same experience Lester Sumrall experienced.

The LORD also told me that Wigglesworth's beloved Polly had to ask him to stop raising her from the dead. She actually told Wigglesworth, *Next time let me go to heaven without delay!*


### Lord May We Become The People Who Will Stand Firm Align In One Accord And Restore One Another

After a lifetime of thinking we need another revival it's not easy to accept the truth as quoted by Kathryn Kuhlman during the meetings at Oral Roberts University in 1974: *It's not Revival; It's Restoration!*

However, once we choose life in Christ, Christ truly does reside in our heart. As believers, we should not require CPR or the 'blue cart' in the emergency room to keep us 'alive with Christ'.

How will you reply to people crying out to God for God to 'do it for them' and especially when they say, *"God send revival."*

Now that you know the truth, will you share the truth with them? I trust you will!

## Chapter 14    Wigglesworth, Unity and Discipleship Books

The LORD prepared mighty plans before I returned to Macon.

During the drive South, the LORD revealed He arranged a one week break for me to attend a cousin reunion in Nebraska.

Upon my return to Georgia, the LORD prompted me to prepare the *In Search of Wigglesworth* portion of *It's A Faith Walk!* within the structure of a separate book.

The book was released on September 23, Yom Kippur.

Five days later, editing was complete and *In One Accord* was released on September 28, The Feast of Tabernacles.

This was a complete shock!

When I questioned the LORD about the switch since *In One Accord* was ninety percent ready before I went to the mountaintop, the LORD reminded me that He was rebuilding my faith and belief to command so the resistance I experienced while trying to bring the believers together in unity would not interfere with the release of the book. Wow.

Without hesitation, the LORD immediately asked me to pull out the discipleship information and prepare a book exclusively about discipleship.

Without realizing it, I questioned the LORD about having a good cover photo which would express the process of discipleship exactly as I questioned the ability to have a good photo for the unity book.

Within about three minutes, the LORD provided the title and subtitle when He provided the photo.

*A Peculiar People: Discipleship of Peculiar People by Peculiar People.* The scripture reference provided is **I Peter 2:9.**

The book was prepared. The cover was approved. The editing was completed so the book could be released 14 days after *In Search of Wigglesworth.*

A call came in from Benny Hinn's ministry team and I was invited to a taping in California. Within 24 hours a flight was arranged and I had less than six 'during the night' hours to pack and arrive at the airport shuttle location in Macon.

## Two Year Anniversary Trip

The LORD confirmed, *I arranged this trip for your anniversary* after my plane landed in San Diego in October 2015.

Within 24 hours of receiving an invitation to a Benny Hinn taping the LORD arranged the flight ticket about 10:30 the evening before my 4:30 shuttle to the Atlanta airport.

It was a surprise trip which was not shared with any of my prayer warriors due to the late night timing of the arrangements. Grateful for the immediate provision while I was surprised to realize I was already in Georgia for two years. Time had flown by!

The LORD helps me 'gain His perspective' when I remain close to Him and proceed upon His step by step assignments. The trip was for His purpose and not arranged to merely be part of the Benny Hinn taping.

The LORD positioned my reserved seat next to a dear man and woman of God on Monday evening.

As soon as Benny Hinn entered the studio, he asked me why it had been so long … when I said Harald Bredesen arranged the invitation in 2006, we focused upon our mutual friend and amazing man of God.

## Message: Palestine Recognized

### Flag Flown at the United Nations Headquarters

Benny Hinn shared that Benjamin Netanyahu always said *No* when border changes were submitted by Palestine, however, he was saying *Maybe* during his recent interview.

Benny confirmed a new flag and land changes were being recognized for Palestine by the United Nations.

The LORD immediately prompted me to research a 9/11 press release for Palestine and I found one, dated September 10.

The LORD confirmed the nations were only given the option to sign or experience a 9/11.

The United Nations press release confirmed enough nations signed to recognize Palestine as a member and the Palestinian flag will be raised at the UN Headquarters as of September 30, 2015.

Wow. When we experienced a 9/11, I did not realize another reason beyond the media stating it was a 911 warning to America. However, the attack date is critical date to Islam. Muslims were attacked on 9/11 in the 1500's and they were attacked three times on 9/11 in the 1600's. Significant coincidence!

## Michelle Corral

The couple seated next to me for the Benny Hinn taping are part of a ministry established by Michelle Corral. They were not going to be able to attend Michelle's meeting on Wednesday evening but, they knew I was supposed to be there.

No idea where the meeting would be held, only that it would be several miles from San Diego. Therefore, I did not think I would be able to go. The LORD immediately arranged for several people to invite me for coffee after the Benny Hinn taping.

It was not clear at first but, they merely wanted to know more about the woman Benny Hinn spoke with.

It was late. Very little time to share details, so they agreed to meet on Wednesday before attending the Michelle Corral meeting in Anaheim together.

### Wednesday: Michelle Corral Meeting

One by one the people canceled. Only one man was available to meet. We set up the location near the Anaheim meeting for 4:30.

On Wednesday, the man was called in to work that night so he had to move our meeting to 2:30. Plus, he needed to meet in Irvine, several miles south of Pastor Michelle's meeting, due to going to work in that area by 5 PM.

Feeling a lot of resistance but, the LORD said *Yes* before I was able to respond.

### Starbucks Moment Turns Into Supernatural Experience!

While the man was parking in the garage, a ministry car pulled up next to his car. Lee Benton, a Pastor and TV Host who utilizes the same CBS Studio location in Los Angeles as Kathryn Kuhlman was with her friend, LeaAnn Pendergrass, a fellow Pastor and TV Host in Los Angeles. Lee began singing: *Jesus, Jesus, Jesus.* Aaron Gowens, my friend, also a pastor, joined Lee in his deep 'Ving Rhames' voice. They finished the phrase together.

Lee became excited to meet a Christian man in the parking garage. She wanted to know what he was doing there in the middle of the afternoon. Aaron shared the fact that he was meeting with me for coffee.

Immediately when Lee heard my name, she started telling Aaron about seeing me on a national Christian TV program.

Aaron was shocked. Lee knew facts that he did not hear on Monday night during or after the Benny Hinn taping. Lee insisted that as soon as I arrive, Aaron needed to interrupt a lunch they were having with a famous film / TV producer.

Immediately, Lee became excited and grabbed my hand. She insisted that she saw me on a Christian TV network program so I responded: *TBN* as I have been on *Praise the Lord* a few times.

She said: *No. Not TBN, CBN. It was not the other interview people with you, it was Pat Robertson. But I do not see much cable TV, so I do not know the name of the program.*

I was in shock 'in the natural' as I whispered, *700 Club?* Lee said: *Yes. It was in the right corner and your name was across the bottom. The interview was about the miracle of the ten books being released in quick succession and your willingness to take on topic by topic.*

Lee started snapping her fingers each time she stated the word topic. Then, she said: *I hope it's OK if I give you the download I'm receiving from the LORD. He's confirming because you are willing to take on the topics, there are 50 more. Is that OK with you?*

Book number ten was 'only a thought' when I was invited to California. Nothing was written so it was not ready for release!

While I was asking the LORD how to respond to Lee, He merely provided the words, *It has not aired yet.*

This is the truth, because number ten was not written or released. Therefore, the interview has not been taped.

This phrase was repeated a few times because she knew a lot of facts about an interview which has not been taped.

The two TV hosts and the producer kept saying what an honor it was to meet me.

She shared how she looked everywhere to find me … she was speaking a mile a minute.

While she held my hand and continued praying, the other TV host handed me her studio card and invited me to be interviewed on her program.

Then Richard, the producer, took my other hand and said, *Thank you.* Before I could ask why, he said, *I want to thank you … really, God wants me to thank you … God has already confirmed this by releasing the books on the high holy days* (Yom

Kippur and Feast of Tabernacles) … *You have been willing to tell the people the truth … you are teaching the people to honor the Sabbath … I am honored to be the one God is speaking through to thank you because it means a lot to me since I am a Messianic Jew …* (more compliments stated, as he held my hand).

None of these details were publicly known. They would not know any of these facts 'in the natural'.

None of the interviews about the books had aired, yet.

Number ten book was not written, edited or released yet.

Aaron was speechless.

The day started out to be an average day. He merely wanted to talk with the woman Benny Hinn spoke to on Monday night.

However, due to this experience and Monday night with Benny Hinn, Aaron canceled his plans to go to work once he realized what he witnessed, *the supernatural series of events and messages divinely orchestrated by our LORD before they occur 'in the natural'.*

Aaron was a key to the orchestration! He was prompted by the LORD to change the location from Anaheim to Irvine Spectrum to be 'closer to work'; he was prompted to change the time from 4:30 to 2:30. The LORD orchestrated so much, Aaron was in awe!

**Michelle Corral Meeting**

Aaron was also blessed by the special word for me from Michelle Corral that evening.

Michelle only called out one person to come forward. She wanted to know who the one person is in a single ministry, a person the world has tried to destroy.

Then she motioned for me to come forward.

The moment she took my hands in hers, she said: *The Lord is confirming your breakthrough is immediately before you.*

After praying more, she said: *The world has taken everything from you, even your home ... many times ... you are going to be restored ... God is bringing your home back to you ...* I knew nothing else about Michelle, beyond the fact she was with Rex Humbard, Pat Boone, and Benny Hinn at Melodyland years ago.

**History details:**

**CBN:** Pastor Harald Bredesen was arranging an interview with **Pat Robertson** (Harald was on the board of CBN) shortly before he fell and passed away in December 2006. He is dearly missed.

**This is Your Day:** A couple of months prior, Pastor Harald also arranged an invitation for a TV interview with **Benny Hinn.** Harald was also on the board of Benny Hinn's ministry.

After the microphone sound check, TBN called.

TBN sent Dr. Nasir Sidikki.

The LORD immediately confirmed I was there to become His witness. Within moments, I became the only witness who heard

171

Pastor Benny share a prophetic word on his program months before (New Year's Eve) regarding a Muslim man converting and bringing his testimony to the program, and his name shall be Nasir. Pastor Harald truly enjoyed the 'switch' in God's plans that evening because he was part of *the LORD's supernatural, divine orchestration!*

Pastor Harald is credited with founding the Charismatic movement globally; known as **"Mr. Charisma"** and yet, remaining as a Lutheran pastor. He knew the world accomplished as much as they could to destroy me many times, before we even had a conversation about these facts.

The destruction has continued during the decade since Pastor Harald transitioned to heaven in 2006. But no matter how much the world does to steal, kill, and destroy my life, Christ, my Yeshua Hamashiach is with me and the Father, Yahweh, never leaves me nor forsakes me. So what I need to do is keep walking forward in faith, speaking truth so all who have ears to hear and eyes to see will be awakened in these days!

Again, the LORD was re-building my faith and belief in order to be ready to command the next steps 'into being' in the region.

His promises are confirmed in the strengthening of our faith!

Upon my return to Georgia, the LORD prompted me to expand the information on prayer and to structure a separate book which was released within a few days, *Always Speak Life.*

It is tough to see what we say about our life as a Christian. Not only within a page or portion of a Sunday bulletin, within Facebook posts and email newsletters from individuals or ministries.

**Example:** A mother inserted a request to pray for her son. Even though he feels encouraged in the morning, by the time he returns from school the enemy has beaten him down again to the point of feeling defeated. She wanted everyone to pray for her son.

LORD forgive us when we know not what we do!

For we are what Your word says we are: **More than conquerors, the head and not the tail, and joint heirs with Christ who defeated the enemy.**

The LORD knew the next part of the plan He was going to reveal would require extensive prayer due to the material He was going to share with me while preparing the next book.

<u>2014-2015</u>: While I have been in Georgia, the LORD has arranged for the release of ten Christian books; five in 2014; five in 2015.

<u>2016</u>: Four more are planned. Three in the editing process. They were placed 'on hold' when this book took the priority position.

*May the truth shared within these pages bless you, fill you to overflowing, and cause you to share it with all members of your family, extended family, all friends, fellow believers, and those who seek the truth and want a relationship with the only living LORD, Yahweh the Father, Yeshua the Son, and the Holy Spirit.*

*May all in your household, family and extended family, be able to declare: As for me and my house, we will serve the LORD!*

*Lord we are grateful that you have given us Your truth in Your Word. We are thankful You reveal it to us, for we do know You sent Your Son to us 'in the world' as the Savior, the Prince of Peace, the Word, the Way, the Truth and the Light.*

## Chapter 15    Two More Books: Prayer and Christmas

As soon as I returned from California the LORD prompted me to prepare a book specifically on Prayer. Each time I ask the people where is God in your situation? They are not able to respond.

The truth is if we only go to God in prayer when we are in trouble. Since that is the case, we need to realize we are in trouble!

*Always Speak Life* has become a theme since I am often asked to pray for family members experiencing health issues and the family typically cautions me to not pray if the person is going to die anyway.

What? Shocked the first few times I heard this status.

However, it is how we have become as a body of Christ.

We align and unite in trauma, in fear based details, in doubt and unbelief that the person will be healed. When we do this, we are forgetting the tactics of the enemy, fear, doubt and unbelief. With his strategy being clear, to steal, kill and destroy.

We ONLY have life in Christ and our life is on earth and in heaven with Christ. Therefore, when we pray *Always Speak Life!*

The book was released on November 15, 2015.

The script about my life story was edited and sent to the producer in Savannah, Georgia on November 30, 2015.

It was midnight on December 1, 2015. I remember it well.

Lights were out. Alarm was set for 5:40 AM.

The LORD told me to remember to research soul invict us. That is what I heard the LORD say so I turned on the light and I wrote it down. I turned out the light and laid back down.

The LORD said invict is not a word. I turned on the light and I reminded Him I had an early morning with a lot of driving. Then, I told Him I was tired but, I promised Him I would look it up when I woke up in the morning. I turned the light out and laid down, again.

Then, the LORD said it was all about Constantine. I thanked Him for the clue and closed my eyes.

The LORD told me to remember sir ya. It did not make sense either but, I turned on the light. I wrote down the words and asked if it was sir Yah for Yahweh or just sir ya.

Silence. After waiting a few moments, I turned out the light and laid down once again.

The next morning the LORD confirmed a book about Christmas was important. Trusting it was separate from Constantine and the terms; however, I was very wrong.

## Restoration Requires Knowledge

## We Perish For The Lack of Knowledge, Hosea 4:6

## We Lack Knowledge of Paganism

## We Have Participated With Paganism

## We Were Warned

## When we Come to Christ, We Are Not To Do As Gentiles Do

The LORD prompted me to watch a program on a history channel about a cemetery in Jerusalem. Moments after I found the program, the LORD told me the truth would be revealed.

A global evangelist desired to be buried in a Jewish cemetery in Jerusalem. The problem: *He wanted to be the first Gentile buried in a Jewish cemetery.*

If the man was Gentile, he was not a Christian!

The bible warns many times: 'Do not to do as the Gentiles do' once we come to Christ. Believe, declare, and learn who we are as Christians grafted into the Jewish family of the LORD.

The LORD pointed out the truth as to why His people perish for the lack of knowledge.

We do not realize Gentiles worshiped other gods.

Gentiles were into sun worship and paganism!

Today we deal with both **Paganism** and **Neo-Paganism.**

**Paganism** is a religion of nature. Pagans revere nature.

Important to realize we are participating with Paganism within the church when we celebrate Christmas and Easter, the holidays Constantine aligned with since he worshiped the sun god. The emperors worshiped Sol Invictus, the image of their god was on their rings and it was on the coins issued during each reign.

While researching the facts the LORD was sharing with me, He prompted me to add specific details regarding **Neo-Paganism.**

I did not have knowledge of **Paganism,** let alone **Neo-Paganism, Modern Paganism, or Contemporary Paganism.**

The groups of all contemporary pagan religious movements derived from the various historical pagan beliefs and they are referred to as the modern 're-awakening' of those who revere nature. They celebrate their beliefs and their religion in both private and public rituals.

Constantine is the connection within the warning in scriptures to not cut down, bring into the home and decorate the (Christmas) tree or ornament it with silver and gold or participate within the celebration (Christmas) as the pagans or gentiles do because it is rooted in pagan worship of the sun gods and Winter Solstice.

**Jeremiah 10. Idols and the True God**

Hear the word which the Lord speaks to you, O house of Israel.

2 Thus says the Lord: *"Do not learn the way of the Gentiles;*

*Do not be dismayed at the signs of heaven,*

*For the Gentiles are dismayed at them.*

3 *For the customs of the peoples are futile;*

*For one cuts a tree from the forest,*

*The work of the hands of the workman, with the ax.*

4 *They decorate it with silver and gold;*

*They fasten it with nails and hammers*

*So that it will not topple.*

5 *They are upright, like a palm tree,*

*And they cannot speak;*

*They must be carried,*

*Because they cannot go by themselves.*

*Do not be afraid of them,*

*For they cannot do evil,*

*Nor can they do any good."*

6 Inasmuch as *there is* none like You, O Lord

(You *are* great, and Your name *is* great in might),

7 Who would not fear You, O King of the nations?

For this is Your rightful due.

For among all the wise *men* of the nations,

And in all their kingdoms,

*There is* none like You.

8 But they are altogether dull-hearted and foolish;

A wooden idol *is* a worthless doctrine.

9 Silver is beaten into plates;

It is brought from Tarshish,

And gold from Uphaz,

The work of the craftsman

And of the hands of the metalsmith;

Blue and purple *are* their clothing;

They *are* all the work of skillful *men.*

**10 *But the Lord is the true God;***

***He is the living God and the everlasting King.***

***At His wrath the earth will tremble,And the nations will not be able to endure His indignation.***

**11 Thus you shall say to them:**

*"The gods that have not made the heavens and the earth shall perish from the earth and from under these heavens."*

**12 *He has made the earth by His power,***

***He has established the world by His wisdom,***

***And has stretched out the heavens at His discretion.***

**13 When He utters His voice,**

***There is* a multitude of waters in the heavens:**

*"And He causes the vapors to ascend from the ends of the earth. He makes lightning for the rain, He brings the wind out of His treasuries."*

**14 *Everyone is dull-hearted, without knowledge;***

***Every metalsmith is put to shame by an image;***

***For his molded image is falsehood,***

***And there is no breath in them.***

**15 *They are futile, a work of errors;***

***In the time of their punishment they shall perish.***

**16 *The Portion of Jacob is not like them,***

***For He is the Maker of all things,***

***And Israel is the tribe of His inheritance;***

***The Lord of hosts is His name.***

***The Coming Captivity of Judah***

**17** Gather up your wares from the land,

O inhabitant of the fortress!

**18** For thus says the Lord:

*"Behold, I will throw out at this time*
*The inhabitants of the land,*
*And will distress them,*
*That they may find it so."*

**19** Woe is me for my hurt!
My wound is severe.
But I say, "Truly this *is* an infirmity,
And I must bear it."

**20** My tent is plundered,
And all my cords are broken;
My children have gone from me,
And they *are* no more.
*There is* no one to pitch my tent anymore,
Or set up my curtains.

**21** *For the shepherds have become dull-hearted,*
*And have not sought the Lord;*
*Therefore they shall not prosper,*
*And all their flocks shall be scattered.*

**22** Behold, the noise of the report has come,
And a great commotion out of the north country,
To make the cities of Judah desolate, a den of jackals.

**23 O Lord, I know the way of man *is* not in himself;**
***It is* not in man who walks to direct his own steps.**

**24** O Lord, correct me, but with justice;
Not in Your anger, lest You bring me to nothing.

**25** *Pour out Your fury on the Gentiles, who do not know You,*
*And on the families who do not call on Your name;*
*For they have eaten up Jacob,*
*Devoured him and consumed him,*
*And made his dwelling place desolate.*

**Calendar:**

The merger of **Yule / Yuletide pagan worship** with **Christmas** occurred when **Constantine** changed the calendar from the Hebrew calendar which included the feasts and festivals which were observed by The Messiah while He was on earth and He set the example for us.

In 300 AD when the Hebrew calendar was dismissed and the merger took place, the Council of Nicaea, controlled by Constantine, merged Christian details and overlapped them on pagan festivals and holidays.

Over time, the Church of Rome stated the merger was good for the people because it would help to evangelize the pagans.

We have been 'out of sync' with our honoring of the only one, true living LORD since the 300s!

### Pagan Worship Merger with Christianity
### Results In Pagan Worship Within The Church

The connections to pagan worship are significant in America.

The Christmas book was not easy to prepare because it includes significant details which confirm we are not honoring Christ on December 25, we are celebrating the birth days of the sun gods. The book was released December 15, 2015.

# Chapter 16    Georgia Guidestones in Elberton, Georgia

Most people in Georgia do not know about the Guidestones.

Several years ago Dr. David R. Reagan was conducting a *Gospel meeting* in Toccoa, Georgia. The location is close to the mountaintop location the LORD arranged for me to gain a new perspective.

While he was there, he decided to check on a rumor he heard about the granite monument erected near Elberton, Georgia.

He was informed the 'guiding force' for the Guidestones was the Lucis Trust headquartered in the United Nations building in New York. This is the same Lucis Trust the LORD revealed to

Gary Kah because it became the publishing entity of public school textbooks.

Are you aware of the Georgia Guidestones?

They are an international tourist attraction promoted as America's Stonehenge even on BBC Television in Europe.

The title does not reveal what the stones include due to Georgia being added to the title. The stones reveal the ten commandments which are considered the satanic commandments. Immediately, you will recognize the connection between the ten commandments listed on the Guidestones and pagan rituals (traditions celebrated by many Christians during the Easter, Ishtar and Christmas holidays) and their beliefs regarding the focus upon nature.

The granite monument was unveiled in 1980 and it displays four Guidestones in eight specific languages.

The languages are: English, Spanish, Swahili, Hindi, Hebrew, Arabic, Chinese, and Russian.

**NOTE: Regarding the languages selected.**

The LORD provided so much truth to 'connect the dots' it was nearly 4 AM when the LORD revealed these facts.

Funny but, it did not seem that late!

The Georgia Guidestones were unveiled in 1980.

The LORD was directing me to research to new, global monetary / currency structure: BRIC.

BRIC was formed in 2008. South Africa insisted they are to be part of the structure; added in 2010. Structure changed to BRICS.

**The languages are an exact match to BRICS!**

**New Global Currency / Monetary Structure:**

New global financial structure is simply referred to as **BRIC**:

1. **Brazil** (Spanish and English),

2. **Russia** (Russian and English),

3. **India** (Hindi and English), and

4. **China** (Chinese and English).

5. **South Africa** (Swahili and English) recently insisted the country was supposed to be included and this resulted in the the name change from **BRIC** to **BRICS**.

**BRICS** established as BRIC in 2008 is the acronym for an association of five major emerging national economies: Brazil, Russia, India, China, and South Africa. Originally the first four were grouped as 'BRIC', before the controversial addition of South Africa in 2010.

### Dr. David R. Reagan Confirmed Lucis Trust
### Headquartered within United Nations Building
### United Nations Plaza in New York
### The New Age Movement

Dr. David Reagan research: According to the rumor, the monument had been paid for by a mysterious group affiliated with the New Age Movement, an international amalgamation of *Humanist societies* whose aim is to prepare the way for the coming of 'Lord Maitreya', a Messiah who will save the world. *The guiding force behind the movement is the Lucis Trust* located at the United Nations Plaza in New York. Reagan confirmed the movement has been well documented in Constance Cumby's book *The Hidden Dangers of the Rainbow.*

**Guidestones Message:** *Let these be Guidestones to an Age of Reason* is carved into the four sides of the capstone in four ancient languages: Classical Greek (dialect of less than 5,000 people located along the Black Sea), Sanskrit (India), Babylonian (sun god worshipers) and Egyptian Hieroglyphs (sun god worshipers; found in caves in America, even in Oklahoma, dating back more than 3500 years).

The Guidestones are located just East of the Hartwell Highway on Guidestones Road out in the country about nine miles north of the center of Elberton, Georgia.

The granite slabs are 19 feet, 3 inches, positioned at the highest point in Elbert County, about 90 miles east of Atlanta, Georgia.

Ten messages align directly to pagan/Baal focus upon nature:

1. Maintain humanity under 500,000,000 in perpetual balance with nature.

2. Guide reproduction wisely – improving fitness and diversity.

3. Unite humanity with a living new language.

4. Rule passion – faith – tradition – and all things with tempered reason.

5. Protect people and nations with fair laws and just courts.

6. Let all nations rule internally resolving external disputes in a world court.

7. Avoid petty laws and useless officials.

**8.** Balance personal rights with social duties.

**9.** Prize truth – beauty – love – seeking harmony with the infinite.

**10.** Be not a cancer on the earth – Leave room for nature – Leave room for nature.

If you have an opportunity to visit the Guidestones I trust the LORD will prompt you to observe but, **<u>do not touch</u>**.

This was also His exact warning to each of us, and to Nancy Haney the prophet from Alaska.

The LORD shared the same warning with me when I was able to view the Guidestones, four days after meeting Nancy and receiving a powerful confirming word through her from the LORD about the merging of the believers, uniting the believers of the many groups.

We did not touch the stones or the description stone to the left of the stones as we entered the area in January 2015 or in June 2016.


**Deceit Evident Within The Church:**

While in deep prayer with the LORD about what is happening in America, regarding the depth of deception many in the body of Christ appear to be 'encased within' the LORD prompted me to check on the Press Release for the Presbyterian Church.

This was a new type of request from the LORD!

In July, the LORD drew my attention to a press announcement regarding the apology issued to any who may be offended by the prayer conducted during the annual meeting of the Presbyterian Church USA.

Not sure how long I sat at the computer viewing the press article with tears flowing due to ancestors coming to America from Scotland long ago for religious and financial freedom.

The basis of the Presbyterian church is the Church of Scotland.

## Presbyterian Church USA Prays to Allah, Calls Muhammad a Prophet

**July 1, 2016. THE Presbyterian Church, USA, is raising eyebrows after lifting up prayers to Allah at its General Assembly meeting last week.**

"Allah bless us and bless our families and bless our Lord. Lead us on the straight path—the path of all prophets: Abraham, Ishmael, Isaac, Moses, Jesus, and Muhammad."

These were the words that rang out over the congregation at The General Assembly of the Presbyterian Church, USA meeting in Portland, Oregon. Wajidi Said, co-founder of the Muslim Education Trust, led the attendees in the prayer to the Islamic deity —a move arranged by the Ecumenical and Interfaith ministry staff at the assembly.

The prayer was part of the "first order of business" during the meeting's opening session, a time dedicated to praying for those affected by the Orlando shooting that occurred just weeks before.

**"In the name of Allah, the beneficent, the merciful, let us praise the Lord … Peace be upon them and peace be upon Allah," Said prayed. He also prayed peace on the "bigots" and "Islamaphobes."**

*LORD so many have been deceived without realizing it so we thank You for keeping Your hand upon us in these days and we ask You just as Stephen asked You to not hold their sin against them and Christ asked You from the cross to forgive those who know not what they do for so many are deceived in this hour in our history.*

## Chapter 17    Americans Are At Choice

### Choose Liberty & Freedom, For The Sake Of America

The mysteries are uncovered and revealed which were hidden from the believers since 300 AD, when Constantine placed us back in time to the pagan worship structure as established by Nimrod.

Everything was different for America!

What did the Pilgrims know? Why were they called Puritans?

What did they bring? They knew the truth!

They sacrificed ALL to bring Liberty and Freedom to America.

They were aware of the lies. They knew the truth, the word.

They knew the truth about pagan worship and it's affects upon their life and their family. They knew what happened when Government decided how the people could worship. They knew what was required to pass truth from generation to generation.

They knew if one generation would tolerate and compromise with the pagan rituals and worship then the next generation would embrace pagan worship as truth and pass on the lies vs. the truth.

The church, the fellowship of the believers, has not united in the truth. Many groups form within the church and the people within the groups become united for an individual cause and they see it through to completion. Sad but true, we have Christ as our cause and our truth as Christians and yet, we have not united.

Because the truth sets us free, the Pilgrims chose to not participate in pagan worship and rituals.

What have we known about the Pilgrims? We were told they were Puritans as though it was the curse. Clearly, we did not realize what it meant! They brought the pure truth to America!

Puritans who lived in prior centuries lived by the word of the LORD. They knew the word establishes liberty and freedom vs. how people attending church today are influenced and affected by the world more than the word.

What is the key difference? Since the Word is true, **Isaiah 59:2** helps us realize the difference: *iniquity separates us from God.*

**Joshua 24:15** confirms we are at choice.

What is the choice?

We can either worship and honor the gods of the past, the gods in the world, or we can choose to honor and worship the only living LORD and declare: … *as for me and my house, we will serve the LORD.*

A good DVD regarding the path, purpose and passion which brought the Pilgrims, the Puritans, to America in 1620 is: *Monumental* **by Kirk Cameron.** The Pilgrims knew what was required to live by faith and to retain our morality, education and laws to secure our freedom and liberty. The LORD prompted me to share the DVD with key leaders throughout the region and the details are also inserted within the first book, *It's A Faith Walk!*

## Faith Monument

The Faith Monument is a granite monument dedicated in 1889, located within a residential community above Plymouth Rock.

Faith Monument stands 81 feet tall and weighs several ton.

**LIE:** Georgia Guidestones monument is claimed as the tallest, biggest granite monument with slabs 19 feet, 3 inches tall. They are not quite one-fourth the height of the Faith Monument. Guidestones also claim to use the most granite at under 300,000 pounds. The Faith Monument took 70 years to complete and the weight is several ton. The truth was known about the Faith Monument for an entire century before the Guidestones were unveiled in 1980, more than 90 years after the Faith Monument was dedicated, 100 years after it was completed.

**Faith Monument**

Faith monument includes four separate sections which display images confirming exactly how we can proceed to retain our liberty and freedom:

**Faith** is at the top of the monument. She points to Heaven, to our Creator. She is holding an open bible, the basis of our faith.

**1. Morality** is holding the Ten Commandments in her left hand and the scroll of revelation in her right hand. At the base of the throne are the engravings: **Evangelist** and **Prophecy.** She has no eyes. She looks inward because liberty must be in us before it will show up within the nation.

**2. Law** founded upon the bible, the source of truth as the Pilgrims **General Laws** confirm: *...by how much they (the laws) are derived from, and agreeable to the ancient Platform of God's Law."* The two carved items under the throne where **Law** is seated represent **Justice** and **Mercy.**

**3. Education** is holding an open book of knowledge, the Bible. Her throne has two carvings: **Youth** receiving instruction and **Wisdom** represented by a grandfather who points to the bible while standing a globe, confirming both parents and grandparents are to teach the youth from a Biblical perspective. She is wearing a **Victory** wreath for focusing the youth upon the truth and the way to proceed in their life, resulting in the *training up a child in the way he shall go so when he is old he will not depart from it* as confirmed within **Proverbs 22:6.**

**4. Liberty** is seated with a sword in his hand. He is prepared to protect the family and liberty. Two carvings: **Tyranny** and **Peace.** The images clearly confirm why the Pilgrims / Puritans were known as the *Parents of America, the Republic* confirmed by the the Founding Fathers.

## Constitutional Convention

As the Founding Fathers were leaving the Constitutional Convention in Philadelphia, Mrs. Powell asked a simple question: *What have you given us Dr Franklin?* She received a simple response from Benjamin Franklin: *A Republic, if you can keep it.*

The plan to retain America as a Republic is confirmed in our founding documents and the Pledge of Allegiance: *... and to the Republic for which it* (the flag) *stands*. A Republic government is of, by and for the people. Each citizen has rights as a sovereign. In a Democracy, rights are granted to and secured by majority rule.

*When the people fear the government there is tyranny,*

*when the government fears the people there is liberty.*

**Quote by Thomas Jefferson**

The constitutional convention is important to Georgia with a key person participating who would make a huge difference within the future plans from Macon, Georgia to Moravian Falls, North Carolina. The man attending was Benjamin Hawkins.

## Structure of America

In fact, the Pilgrims are credited with establishing the structure for many states: *... they colonized many of the states.*

*More than half of the Founding Fathers and the signers of the Declaration of Independence were seminary graduates!*

Many of the signers helped to fund the cost for Congress to print and distribute the first 10,000 bibles.

Bibles were provided for every church, school, and family in America (research by David Barton).

**Bradford Quote.** On the Faith Monument, a special quote from William Bradford speaks to the depth of faith, knowledge, and wisdom in the people we refer to as Pilgrims or Puritans:

*Thus out of small beginnings greater things have been produced by His hand that made all things of nothing and gives being to all things that are, and as one small candle may light a thousand, so the light here kindled hath shone unto many, yea in some sort to our whole nation, let the glorious name of Jehovah have all praise.*

Bradford focused all praise on the Hebrew name of our LORD, the Father, Jehovah our Yahweh, Yah or Y-h (vowels not used), the praises to the one true and only living God. Hallelujah means 'praise Yah'. God be praised, worship of Jehovah / Yahweh, Yah.

With everything based upon the Word, the Bible, and the exact details being provided to keep a nation free and a people living in liberty, how could a blessed nation return to the traditions of pagan worship and the pagan rituals of Christmas and Easter?

Instead of following our Hebrew calendar which includes the structure the LORD put in place, we denied the truth after receiving so many benefits from the Christian standard set in America by the Pilgrims / Puritans.

### If The Structure Was Already In Place, What Happened?

Truth was not passed from generation to generation so we did not proceed per the structure which would secure and pass on liberty and freedom from generation to generation.

Plus, America also removed the ban Pilgrims placed upon worship of the sun god, the Sunday pagan worship and rituals which were not celebrated for nearly 250 years (1620 to mid-1800's). This means the people and churches realigned with paganism about 250 years after the ban was placed upon paganism in America. Extensive immigrant infusion from Europe in the early to mid-1800's influenced this change. States were established coast to coast and land that was taken from Native Americans was promoted as 'tax free' for the immigrants from many nations.

## We Tolerated & Compromised
## Next Generation Embraced Without Knowledge
## Tradition Passed On As Truth vs. Truth Becoming Tradition

The truth about the plan for America to be a blessed nation and to remain as a blessed nation, living in liberty and freedom, separate and set apart from the rule of a Monarch over the church and the people was 'lost in translation'.

**Hosea 4:6.**

**My people are destroyed (perish) for lack of knowledge.**

**Because you have rejected knowledge,**

**I also will reject you from being priest for Me;**

**Because you have forgotten the law of your God,**

**I also will forget your children.**

We did not seek the LORD's truth.

Success and wealth goals resulted in power and greed expanding in all parts of society. Acceptance of the 'value' of Christians became linked with 'assets and credit (debt) worthiness'. Public education became the norm vs. continuing with education based upon Christian values. Government made the decisions and churches have to comply in England. Now, it is the same in America.

When Christians are questioned, they have to supply a 'politically correct' response and report all transactions to the government for government review and approval as a corporation.

So much of what has happened is rooted in <u>Georgia history</u>!

At this point I felt like I was in a V-8 commercial: ***I could have proceeded with greater speed if I would have been 'armed with the truth'.*** This is why the LORD prompted me to remain in Georgia so He could reveal layer upon layer of the deceit added on top of His truth so He could only reveal one layer to me 'at a time' since it was a lot to take in within a few weeks or a few months!

What do we need to know and do to help turn it around? We must begin by:

1. Seeking the truth and choosing truth vs. tradition.
2. Become indefatigable (persistently tireless) with the LORD.
3. Seek Restoration for the body of Christ with truth 'in hand'.

### Separation of Church and State

The truth is not understood by many Americans.

Many believe the media and man's interpretation while the truth is the Founding Fathers knew what it was like to have the Government/Monarch control the people and their rights to fellowship. They knew the government should not come between the people and the LORD.

They set up the Separation of Church and State because they did not want the President in America to become the head of the church and control what people could believe.

The Pilgrims / Puritans brought the standard for retaining liberty and freedom to America. They actually structured the government for each of the colonies. They knew the truth: The

LORD's word and living a life according to the word is what retains liberty and freedom.

Christians have remained separate from all political positions for so long and have not wanted Christians to 'become embroiled within the political system'. Therefore, it is absolutely a mystery why we should think any political positions are going to be held by deep men and women of God!

LORD thank you for keeping Your hand upon us!


**Republic of America.** America was established as a Republic form of Government. Citizens select representatives who would proceed of, by and for the people because a Republic secures the individual, sovereign rights of each citizen.

America has always required our full involvement in the process. Our Founding Fathers provided individual rights for each of us. The Bill of Rights is 'in addition' to the Declaration of Independence which provides for us to alter the government if the representatives are not protecting our rights. In fact, within the first few words it states if the representatives do not represent us we are required to remove them and replace them with people who will!

*The first requisite of a good citizen in this Republic of ours is that he shall be able and willing to pull his own weight.*
New York, Chamber of Commerce, 1902
*The government is us; we are the government, you and I.*
Asheville, North Carolina, 1902

*Our country, <u>this great republic</u>, means nothing unless it means the triumph of a real democracy, the triumph of popular government, and, in the long run, of <u>an economic system under which each man shall be guaranteed the opportunity to show the best that there is in him</u>.* Osawatomie, Kansas, 1910

## Quotes by Theodore Roosevelt, President 1901-1909

Roosevelt was clearly aware of the pressure to become a global democracy. He knew the dangers of departing from individual, sovereign rights to majority rule and socialism. Many citizens are unaware of the timing or the scheme which was arranged by the families who gained control of the leadership and the economy, requiring action steps which changed America from a Republic to a Democracy. Until we gather a 'large crowd' when personal rights are violated, a person saying 'something is not right' is not heard in a majority rule government. Losing our individual, citizen rights secured in a Republic means we lose our voice in America! The facts prove how & when it happened in Chapters 18, 19, and 20.

*May the truth shared within these pages bless you, fill you to overflowing, and cause you to share it with all members of your family, extended family, all friends, fellow believers, and those who seek the truth and want a relationship with the only living LORD, the Father, the Son and the Holy Spirit. May all in your household, family and extended family, be able to declare: as for me and my house, we will serve the LORD! Lord we are grateful that You have given us Your truth in Your Word. We are thankful You reveal it to us, for we do know You sent Your Son to us 'in the world' as the Savior, Prince of Peace, the Word, the Way, the Truth and the Light.*

## Chapter 18    Significance of Macon, Georgia to America

Georgia history was foreign to me.

To my surprise, history facts the LORD has revealed to me were not known by most of the people who have lived in Georgia their entire life. This is why I'm sharing a brief summary of the key facts the LORD has provided to me in chronological, historical order.

### Georgia Named After King George

Oglethorpe was commissioned as a General by King George. He was put in charge of the colony of Georgia. Oglethorpe was a Mason. He sailed to America with several Masons from the UK.

The first settlers in Georgia were from England. Oglethorpe offered to bring the people in the debtors prisons from England to America with the promise they would inhabit the State of Georgia.

Oglethorpe was commissioned as a Brigadier General for his efforts.

Georgia was the last of the 13 British colonies, established in 1732, more than 100 years after the Pilgrims landed at Plymouth Rock in 1620. Pilgrims are credited with the government structure of the colonies in America.

**Benjamin Hawkins, Assigned US Agent to Native Americans by George Washington.**

Generally recognized as an Indian 'agent', Benjamin Hawkins held the title of General Superintendent of all tribes south of the Ohio River for more than two decades.

He was well respected as the overseer of the longest period of peace with the Creek, only to watch his lifetime of work destroyed by a faction of this Indian Nation known as the 'Red Sticks' during the War of 1812 which was being fought against the British and the 'Red Sticks' war extended through 1813 and 1814.

Definition within Wikipedia: *The term "red sticks" was derived from their red-colored war clubs and the ceremonial red sticks used by Creek medicine men. This faction was made up mostly of Creek of the Upper Towns, who supported traditional leadership and culture, including the preservation of communal land for cultivation and hunting. It was a time of increasing pressure on Creek territory by European-American settlers. Creek of the Lower Towns, who were closer to the settlers and had more mixed-race families, had already been forced to make numerous land cessions to the Americans.*

Why were the Creek Indian 'Red Sticks' so upset?

A man named **William Bibb** was 'stealing' the land!

At this time in history, Creek land extended across the nation from coast to coast, and the established states of North and South Carolina and nearly all of Georgia plus the Creek territory would represent nearly all other states which were not identified or established, yet.

Hawkins negotiated the Treaty of Hopewell. The famous peace treaty was negotiated in Hopewell, South Carolina.

Hawkins made his home in Crawford county Georgia which borders **Bibb** county on the West.

An odd historical fact: Fort Benjamin Hawkins is located on the land at the East border of **Bibb** County - Macon, Georgia.

Fort Benjamin Hawkins became the first residential community in Macon Georgia. It was the location of the first homes and the first church built in the region.

After all of the effort of Hawkins to unite the tribes and keep peace with the Creek Indians, the largest tribe north of Mexico, everything changed due to the actions of **William Wyatt Bibb**.

**William Wyatt Bibb.**

Bibb won political favor after obtaining Native American land from the Creek tribe throughout Georgia and Alabama. Truth be told, Bibb proceeded with illegal treaties to remove the Creek from their land. Later, it was realized that he arranged the land grab from the Creek Tribe for cotton cultivation by a plantation owner. Bibb was honored even though he entered into invalid treaties with the Creek Indians and arranged the land for settlers and military.

The Creek tribal leaders proceeded to court with the treaties and a judge confirmed they were invalid but, the land was already settled.

**Cotton Field, Ready to Harvest**

By the time the Creek tribe obtained the resolution within the official American court system, the Creek were unable to return to the land because it was settled; A cotton plantation was already established and the Army occupied Fort Benjamin Hawkins.

Bibb was a State representative. He became a US Congressman and a Senator representing the people of Georgia.

Due to Bibb's successful efforts to also secure the Creek land throughout Georgia and Alabama, he was appointed by President James Monroe as the first governor of the newly established Alabama territory in 1817. Alabama became a State by the end of 1819.

President James Madison served immediately before President Monroe. Famous quote of Madison, ***We have staked our future on our ability to follow the Ten Commandments with all our heart.***

As you can tell, times quickly changed!

President Monroe honored and rewarded Bibb for stealing the land of the Creek tribe.

**Bibb County Georgia and Bibb County Alabama** are named after **William Wyatt Bibb** due to his successful efforts in the complete removal of all Creek Indians off their land in both states.

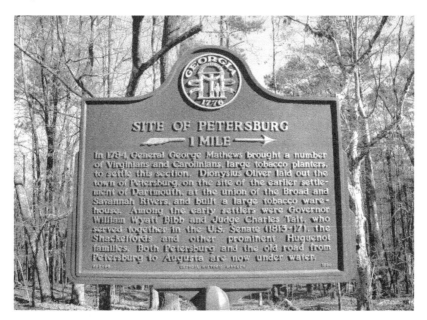

Bibb grew up in Elbert County, near Elberton, Georgia. Elberton became the location selected for the Georgia Guidestones.

**Petersburg.**

The Bibb family lived in the booming town of Petersburg which was located at the connecting point of the Savannah and Broad Rivers. Petersburg was established for new settlers from Virginia and North Carolina to inspect the tobacco plants.

When Bibb finished medical school, he returned to Petersburg as the physician for the region.

The town of Petersburg was built over the ruins of a large Muskogean Creek Native American settlement and town. Many of the Creek burial mounds were leveled to build the town of Petersburg.

The Creek burial mounds included a large spiral mound like the one that still exists as the Creek Temple Mound near Macon, Georgia within the Ocmulgee National Monument.

Petersburg no longer exists.

What was a town at that time is now under Lake Russell.

Petersburg / Lake Russell is close to Elberton, Georgia where the Georgia Guidestones are located.

Depending upon the address in Petersburg or Lake Russell it is within one to eight miles from Elberton, Georgia.

**Creek Indians. Largest tribe north of Mexico.**

Prior to the divisive tactics by Bibb, the Creek tribe was the largest tribe in existence north of Mexico.

The majority of land from coast to coast belonged to the Creek Indians.

Have you ever heard the saying: ***LORD willing and if the Creek don't rise!***

The Creek in this saying does not represent a water creek, it means if the region remains at peace because there will not be an uprising by the Creek Indians before dawn.

The Creek Nation was completely displaced from their fertile land without an option to survive. Bibb knew the treaty was not valid and the Creek Nation was already presenting the treaty in court. Bibb quickly met with Creek men who were not the decision making leaders of the tribe and obtained a second, signed agreement. Even though Bibb was aware the first and second treaties were not valid, he used to proceed with his plans for the land.

The Creek men who signed the second treaty were executed by the tribal council because they operated outside of the tribal structure, tribal procedure and policy, and their area of responsibility.

Bibb was not held responsible. Instead, Bibb was honored. Bibb was appointed Governor of Alabama by the President. Settlers named Bibb County Georgia & Bibb County Alabama after William Wyatt Bibb. The counties remain in his name today.

# The Peace Pipe

Would have been great if the true meaning of the sharing of the peace pipe was realized by the emerging political leadership within the early 1800's.

All regions were 'at peace' with the Pilgrims / Puritans.

Hawkins kept all tribes 'at peace' and retained the longest period of time for the Creek to remain 'at peace'.

A book was shared with me a few years ago which described what we are to do when we receive a gift.

Each gift 'in us' and 'in life' is either honored or not.

The reference to the Peace Pipe explains what happened when European-American settlers established the structure of the states and the Native American gift of the peace pipe was misunderstood.

The Indians trusted they were 'in fellowship' and 'at peace' with the new residents on the land so they gave them a peace pipe to confirm they were going to live 'in unity'. The gift, however, was quickly put into a showcase box and placed on the mantle for 'all guests' to see. It was never touched or used once it was given by the Native Americans to the new settlers.

The same is true for us to this day as Christians. When we do not operate 'in the gifts', we stop or block the flow of the gift(s) in us and the blessings showered upon us, and this is how the same thing happens to us. We become blocked and stuck and we think God put us on a shelf.

**Masons and the Macon, Georgia Connection.**

**American Masonic Order controlled by Illuminati.**

**Documentation confirms control began in July, 1776.**

Extensive research was provided to Gary Kah with the entire chronological history and structure of the Masonic Order and the plans by the Illuminati to control all aspects of life in America: The churches, the businesses, the court systems, the government people and departments or offices, and the financial and economic structure of the states and America exactly when we gained our independence: July, 1776.

**Illuminati, Lucis Trust, United Nations, One World Order**
**World Goodwill, Lifebridge Foundation**
**Trust for Conservation and New Group of World Servers**

Gary Kah's ministry was revealed to me by a Doctor who heard me speak at a church in California in the mid to late 1990's. He invited me to a BBQ after the service.

When I arrived, I offered to help with the BBQ, however, a videotape was in the machine and ready to begin. My instructions were to view the video while my hosts prepared the meal.

Gary's ministry received all of the documentation which confirmed extensive research regarding the 100 year plan established against generations of Americans. It was established by

Alice Bailey, the woman in charge of Lucifer Publishing which was later changed to Lucis Trust Publishing, Lifebridge, etc.

One part of the 100 year plan within the satanic vision Alice Bailey received and acted upon, focused upon affecting future generations. Gary Kah who was prompted by the LORD to research Lucifer Publishing, Lucis Trust regarding publishing and distributing public school textbooks across America.

Content of school textbooks was purposely structured to cause youth to rebel, to disrepect authority, and to be divisive in the family and in the community. This is contrary to the education plan identified on the Freedom Monument. The video includes the specific letters from Alice Bailey who received a vision regarding how to proceed. The letters are on the business stationery of Lucifer Publishing in New York. The firm was challenged due to the title so they changed the name to Lucis Trust. They have printed the text books for the public schools in America.

They have established and operated under various titles, as noted above: World Goodwill, Lifebridge Foundation, and New Group of World Servers, etc. Since the video was prepared about the school textbooks, the United Nations Educate 2000 program distributed the same school textbooks to many nations around the world. Until the LORD prompted someone to share the research of Dr. Reagan, I was not aware of the connection between the Lucis Trust and the Georgia Guidestones.

**Masonic structure linked to Illuminati and Lucis Trust.**

After the material about the textbook publisher was released by Gary, a woman provided extensive historical information about the Masonic change under Illuminati control in America July, 1776.

This is a key point since the same Lucis Trust, Illuminati, and New World Order, and One World Religion are linked and they have more connections with Georgia.

Beyond Lucis Trust Publishing distributing school textbooks, the Trust has become the financial source for maintaining and possibly building the Georgia Guidestones in Elberton, Georgia.

**Christian Voice UK** research obtained the list of names utilized by Lucis Trust and the members of the Lucis Trust foundation division which is known as the *New Group World Servers.* The article refers to Foundation(s) involved as member(s) of New Group World Servers.

## Masonic Structure, Illuminati, New World Order
## Established in Macon, Georgia by Albert Pike

**Albert Pike** was referred to as an imposing individual who was rarely questioned about his motives since he was at least six feet tall and he weighed at least 300 pounds.

Pike easily positioned himself at the top of each organization as you can tell by his biography and due to being in the right place for him to do what he wanted to do.

At the time, Pike was very connected with Masonic 33$^{rd}$ degree contacts globally and he found that he could get away with all of his illegal actions at that time in the history of America.

**Albert Pike** became the founder of the Scottish Rite in America and the Sovereign Grand Commander of the Scottish Rite's Southern Jurisdiction in 1859. He remained in this position for the next 32 years which was the remainder of his life.

### Civil War. Confederate States Capital: Macon.

Goals were clear with Macon, Georgia being the location selected as the new Confederate States capital. The entire arsenal for the Civil War was housed in Macon, Georgia.

### Albert Pike Commissioned Confederate Brigadier General.

Albert Pike was from Boston. He was commissioned as a Confederate Brigadier General in 1861 over the Indian Territories for the Army of the Confederate States. Pike was in charge of the ordering of supplies for the huge territory granted to him as the Brigadier General.

**Albert Pike to be Arrested; Theft of Materials and Funds.**

Within months, in 1862, Pike was on the list to be arrested due to his mishandling of funds and materials; supplies missing from inventory and/or removed from the arsenal in Macon. The arsenal in Macon was specifically arranged for the Confederate States and all supplies were stockpiled in Macon, Georgia.

**Albert Pike Resignation; Released days After his Arrest.**

Pike resigned his position days prior to being arrested on the original charges and additional charges of illegal actions he allowed, crimes committed by his men. Pike's resignation letter was received at about the same time as his arrest. Therefore, Pike was released a few days after he was arrested.

**Albert Pike After the War.**

Pike refocused upon the financial and political structure to control communities, States and America through the Masonic Order. Pike spent significant time in Macon, Georgia.

**Albert Pike becomes Top Leader in Knights of the KKK.**

According to historians, by 1869 Pike was also the top leader in the Knights of the KKK.

**Albert Pike coordinates first attempt at New World Order.**

Pike was supposedly self-appointed as the coordinator of the first attempted structure of a New World Order with the help of his friends.

His right-hand man was from Switzerland, Phileas Walder. Walder was a former Lutheran minister, a Masonic leader who stated within his biography that he was an occultist and a spiritualist.

Pike also worked closely with Giusseppe Mazzini of Italy, a 33rd degree Mason who founded the Mafia in 1860. By the mid-1860's Mazzini was also the leader of the Illuminati globally.

Pike was recognized as the leader of the Illuminati in America.

The 33$^{rd}$ degree is the top Masonic position. Pike gathered only the top leaders globally from the list of 33$^{rd}$ degree Masons to proceed upon his plan for the New World Order.

**Albert Pike, a self-declared Satanist.**

According to the historical summary on Pike, he declared he was a Satanist. He stated he indulged in the occult. He actually confirmed that the bracelet he wore was used to summon Lucifer, with whom Pike said he had constant communication.

As the Grand Master of a Luciferian group known as the Order of the Palladium, or The Sovereign Council of Wisdom, which was founded in Paris in 1737, Pike felt he ruled the New World Order at this point.

Palladium was brought to Greece from Egypt by Pythagoras a Greek philosopher who was known for establishing the Pythagoreanism movement in the fifth century, and it was this cult of Satan that was introduced to the inner circle of the Masonic lodges across America. The Order of the Palladium was aligned with the Palladium of the Templars. Pike established the American headquarters in Charleston, South Carolina with additional offices in Rome, Italy and Berlin, Germany.

**Albert Pike Vision. Letter to Giusseppe Mazzini on August 15, 1871.** Pike received a vision which predicted three world wars which would position the nations for the New World Order, the One World Government.

Pike shared the vision with Mazzini in writing. Pike did not realize Islam is the religion of Muslims. Pike referred to the people of Islam as Moslems throughout the letter to Mazzini.

Brief summary of the vision; prediction of three world wars:

**WWI** required to destroy Tsars (Christian) Russia.

**Goal:** Athiest communism becomes prominent and destroys faith in other religion(s)

**Reality:** Tsar Nicholas II removed March 1917; abdicated the Romanov throne under pressure; Romanov family was arrested; Entire family executed during the night of July 16-17, 1918. **DUMA** established as an advisory group by and for Tsar Nicholas II becomes the founding structure of Communism in Russia under dictatorship rule of Lenin and the Bolsheviks. Russians agreed due to the promise of peace, land, and bread.

By 1922, Russian government was confirmed as a Republic.

The Union of Soviet Socialist Republics (USSR).

NOTE: A Republic form of government secures rights for each sovereign citizen. Russia was not a Republic government of, by and for the people.


<u>**WWII**</u> Fascists (includes Communists and Moslems, per Pike, actually Islamists) will battle against Zionists; Athiest Communism and Moslems/Islamists will become equal to the population of Christianity around the world.

**Reality:** This agenda became the global reality! American pilots, the Flying Tigers, risked everything in 1941-1942 to provide supplies to China during their war with Japan. John Birch was a global missionary from a young age. He served as an intelligence officer, a Captain in the Air Force, during WWII. John realized America supplied and defended China during the war while the American government sanctioned Japan. The attack on Pearl Harbor December 7, 1941, was a direct result of the Empire of

Japan's anger with the decisions of President Roosevelt to supply China and sanction Japan.

By 1949, the Chinese government was under the dictatorship of Mao as The People's Republic of China. However, China was not a Republic government of, by or for the people.

More facts are revealed in Chapter 20.

**WWIII** Political Zionists and leaders of the Moslems/Islamists will battle; both will be conquered and exterminated .

### Albert Pike, established Scottish Rite in Macon.

The Scottish Rite Lodge of Perfection was the first in the nation and it was personally chartered by Albert Pike in 1882.

### Albert Pike and The New and Reformed Palladian Rite.

Together with Mazzini, 33$^{rd}$ degree, Lord Henry Palmerston of England, 33$^{rd}$ degree, and Otto von Bismarck from Germany, 33$^{rd}$ degree, Albert Pike intended to use the Palladian Rite to create a Satanic umbrella group that would tie all Masonic groups together.

Pike is credited himself in his biography to read and write 16 languages. No research is available to confirm this claim. Historians state Pike never confirmed any languages beyond English.

**Masonic Home in Macon.** It was a unique time to be within the complex of buildings of the Masonic Children's Home in Macon, a 650 acre orphanage located on the highest hill in Macon, *The Heart of Georgia*. The cornerstone was laid in 1903. The home was dedicated in 1905. The location is not easily identified as a good environment for children since it does not include anything which would represent a place to gather and enjoy games, sports, or outdoor activities. The buildings are business building structures with a location for young boys on one side and young girls on the other side of the main building. Two separate buildings were built for older boys and older girls located on each side of the main building.

The property does include a swimming pool which is only available during the summer months. When I informed a local Christian fellowship of the bleak environment at the home, a group of men visited the home. They have arranged to 'shoot hoops' with the boys one or two days each week.

It was tough to visit the home, a dark environment. The testimony of the young lady clearly confirmed the enemy was the only voice she was hearing while in the privacy of her room.

Enough about Pike and what he put into place in Macon which is affecting every town and community across America.

Albert Pike is just one man, so is Bibb, and if they can do this much with the enemy as their helper, imagine what each of us can accomplish since **I John 4:4** is our anchor *... He who is in you is greater than he who is in the world.*

May we proceed in each community to do as the LORD requests within the scriptures, *see to the needs of the widows and the orphans.* **James 1:27** *Pure and undefiled religion before God and the Father is this: to visit orphans and widows in their trouble, and to keep oneself unspotted from the world.* As Abraham Lincoln stated during the Civil War, *My concern is not whether God is on our side, my greatest concern is to be on God's side for God is always right.*

**More Decisions Affecting America
During Meetings Which Took Place in Georgia.**

# Chapter 19    Significance of Augusta & Jekyll Island, Georgia

The LORD arranged for me to spend a special day in Augusta. I was in Macon for more than two years when the tour was arranged to see the beautiful, historical churches in Augusta.

While turning to go down a street between churches on both adjoining streets, I noticed something rather odd. The block on Seventh Street only had two large homes which were maintained but, it appeared they were not residences.

When I asked if we could stop a moment since I wanted to know about the two homes, I was told the first home was the childhood home of the former United States President Woodrow Wilson and the second home was the home of a former Supreme Court Justice but, the name was not known.

Shocked. From history classes I remembered Woodrow Wilson was credited with the Industrial Revolution in America while he was the Governor of New Jersey immediately before he became the President.

No idea Woodrow Wilson was linked to Georgia prior to this moment!

During the worship time before the next Rebecca King bible study, the LORD prompted me to check on who lived in the house next door to Woodrow Wilson and when were the IRS and Federal Reserve were established and enacted, and 'the crisis' which preceded the Federal Reserve being established.

The combination of details seemed odd, but I sent a text to myself to check on the details after the bible study.

The LORD is amazing!

**1907.** The banking crisis happened while **President Theodore Roosevelt was in Louisiana on a hunting trip.**

Secretary of the Treasury was eager to make loans to the banks that were solvent. Several of the banking leaders at the time were also members of the Jekyll Island Club located off the coast near Brunswick, Georgia.

Regardless of the involvement of the various bankers from the Jekyll Island Club, J P Morgan appointed himself as the decision maker regarding which banks failed and which ones survived.

**Warning by President Thomas Jefferson**

*If the American people ever allow private banks to control the issue of their currency, first by inflation, then by deflation, the banks and corporations that will grow up around the banks will deprive the people of all property – until their children wake-up homeless on the continent their fathers conquered.*

**Historic Childhood Home of Woodrow Wilson**

Woodrow's father, Joseph Wilson was a chaplain in the Confederate army and used his church, First Presbyterian Church of Augusta as a hospital for injured Confederate troops.

# Historic Home of Supreme Court Justice Lamar

The home next door to the childhood home of Woodrow Wilson was the family home of a boyhood friend of Woodrow Wilson, Supreme Court Justice Joseph Lamar.

Currently the historical society uses the home to arrange the tours of the childhood home of Woodrow Wilson.

**1908.** The people found the appointment of Lamar by President Taft odd since it is rare for a justice to be appointed from the opposing political party. However, the two men were supposedly friends since 1908 when Taft met and played golf with Lamar at the now famous golf course in Augusta, Georgia.

**1910.** Senator Aldrich from Rhode Island researched the banking system in Europe, the system the founding fathers did not allow within the structure of the banking system in America. Aldrich gathered the bankers together, especially those who were members of the Jekyll Island Club, in his personal train car at the New Jersey train station. They journeyed on to Jekyll Island.

**Jekyll Island Club. Jekyll Island, Georgia**

Senator Aldrich called the meeting a 'duck hunt' when he was questioned by the press who met the group at the Brunswick, Georgia train station.

The gathering was referred to as the 'duck hunt' several years after the Federal Reserve was established by the private banker families involved in the meeting.

The Federal Reserve has not become a federal agency within the government of America to this day.

The same men are also credited with establishing the IRS which is also a structure they control privately. The IRS is not a government agency within the government of America, either.

**1910.** Lamar was appointed as Supreme Court Justice.

**1913.** Wilson was recognized for the Industrial Revolution in America while Governor of New Jersey. He was elected President of the United States. Inauguration of Wilson on March 4.

After numerous failed attempts to enact the IRS and Federal Reserve, Wilson signed both the **Federal Reserve Act** and the **Revenue Act** in early 1913. Also, he signed the **Federal Farm Loan Act** and the **Antitrust Act.** To proceed with all of this, two amendments to the Constitution were ratified in 1913:

16$^{th}$ **Amendment** allowed the national government to collect income taxes, a power that was formerly limited to the states; new taxing and spending power, the federal government was able to interfere more in intra-state issues by offering funding if states would voluntarily comply with federal policies.

**17th Amendment.** This amendment took away the power of state legislators to select the Senators to represent the State; receive campaign donations from anywhere, not only the citizens of their state; much stronger incentive to respond to national party politics than to the interests of only their state.

Prior to the 17$^{th}$ Amendment, Senators had to be recognized as 'leaders on behalf of the people's representatives in the state' by fellow Assemblymen or Congressmen. When Senators need to be replaced, State Assembly or Congress would help with the process.

Since State Representatives selected the Senators per the constitution, this kept Senators loyal to their State. The 17$^{th}$ Amendment changed the role of Senators to be focused upon Federal vs. State issues. They became involved in 'global' affairs vs. being focused only on the State projects or requests of the People they represent to benefit the residents of the State.

Questions to ponder:

1. Can we blame Woodrow Wilson?

2. Can we blame the Congress or the Senate?

A quick answer to both questions: **No!**

Within the Declaration of Independence, we the people have the opportunity and the responsibility to counter the actions of the government:

*We hold these truths to be self-evident, that all men are created equal, that they are endowed by their Creator with certain unalienable Rights, that among these are Life, Liberty and the pursuit of Happiness.--That to secure these rights, Governments are instituted among Men, deriving their just powers from the consent of the governed, --That whenever any Form of Government becomes destructive of these ends, it is the Right of the People to alter or to abolish it, and to institute new Government, laying its foundation on such principles and organizing its powers in such form, as to them shall seem most likely to effect their Safety and Happiness.*

Changes enacted by Wilson resulted in American no longer being a Republic as established by the Founding Fathers. Our Republic is confirmed in our Pledge of Allegiance. A Republic structure provides 'sovereign rights to each citizen'. A Democracy is controlled by the majority and the majority holds the rights.

Wilson was recognized as the leading force in the Progressive Movement. Democrats held the majority rule in Congress during Wilson's term.

**1913. Mexico.** Wilson replaced Ambassador Henry Lane Wilson (appointed by President Taft) in Mexico by sending a replacement to Mexico shortly after his inauguration without notifying Ambassador Wilson. This action was taken solely upon the input from a reporter, William Bayard Hale. Ambassador Henry Wilson was officially dismissed by President Wilson on July 17, 1913. He was blamed for 'participating in the coup d'etat' against President Madero.

**1914. Lamar** becomes Supreme Court Justice appointed to commission by Wilson for the negotiation of Mexico dispute.

**1914. Wilson** signs legislation creating the **Federal Trade Commission.**

**1915. Lamar** was forced to leave the bench due to illness. However, he retained his income until his death early in 1916.

**1917. Wilson** is re-elected in March .

**1917. March 15, Tsar Nicholas** abdicated throne in Russia.

**DUMA** was established by Tsar Nicholas as an advisory group. This structure is the basis of what quickly became Fascism or Communism throughout Russia.

**1917. April 6,** America enters WWI with Britain, France, and Russia after Wilson declares to make *"the world safe for democracy."*

**Major shift for America from Republic to Democracy!**

**Wilson** raised income taxes.

**Wilson** borrowed billions from citizens by issuing what the government called Liberty Bonds.

**Wilson** loaned billions to France, Britain, and other allies.

**1917. Espionage Act of 1917. Selective Service Act of 1917.**

**1918. Wilson** pursued until the **Sedition Act** was in place and used the Act along with both the **Espionage and Selective Service Acts of 1917** to suppress all anti-draft activists.

**1919. Wilson** promoted the **League of Nations (United Nations; structure of the One World or New World Order)** with the help of the British Prime Minister George and French Premier Clemencea with the nations signing the Treaty of Versailles.

**Wilson** wins the Nobel Peace Prize for being honored as the leader responsible for ending WWI with the Treaty of Versailles.

At this time, Wilson is publicly credited in global newspapers for creating the League of Nations.

The League of Nations has become The United Nations.

**1920. Former Ambassador to Mexico, Henry Lane Wilson** was the Chair of the Indiana State Chapter of the League to Enforce Peace, a  position he held until after the war. He resigned the State position after the war due to the United States involvement within the League of Nations. Henry Wilson retained his membership within Sons of the American Revolution, Society of Colonial Wars, and Loyal Legion for the rest of his life.

**1921. Wilson's** second term as President ends on March 4.

**Republic of America converted to a Democracy.** What Wilson did to America took us from being a Republic form of government as we were established, of the people, by the people, and for the people, to a Democracy where the majority rules.

Historians agree that the legislation pushed through by Wilson was unparalleled until America experienced the passage of Franklin Roosevelt's **New Deal** in 1933. President Roosevelt considered Woodrow Wilson his 'mentor' even though Wilson died a few years before Roosevelt was elected President.

More facts are revealed in Chapter 20!

### 1921-1924. Confession by Woodrow Wilson.

Near the end of his life, whether it was a death bed confession or not, Wilson admitted *I have unwittingly ruined my country.*

### Alleged Death Bed Confession.

In an alleged death bed confession, Wilson confirmed he was bound by the men who pushed for the legislation to be enacted and the two entities (Federal Reserve and IRS) to be established and therefore to proceed due to their efforts to ensure his election as Governor of New Jersey, his election and re-election as President.

Key portion of his confession: *I am a most unhappy man. I have unwittingly ruined my country. A great industrial nation is controlled by its system of credit... all our activities are in the hands of a few men. We have come to be one of the worst ruled, one of the most completely controlled and dominated Governments in the civilized world, no longer a Government by free opinion, no longer a Government by conviction and the vote of the majority, but a Government by the opinion and duress of a small group of dominant men.*

Enough about Wilson and what he put in place in America!

If one man can influence so many decisions or be influenced by the enemy to proceed upon so many decisions against America, whether it appears he proceeded alone or 'with the help of a friend or two' imagine what one man or woman of God can accomplish since the truth is in the scripture: **I John 4:4. ...** *He who is in you is greater than he who is in the world.*

**Proverbs 22:6**

**Train up a child in the way he should go,**
**And when he is old he will not depart from it.**

# Chapter 20    Significance of Warm Springs, Georgia

**Economy was impacted from a new angle.**

Again, a Georgia location is involved.

Roosevelt's Little White House in Warm Springs, Georgia.

Citizens felt it was 'the best place for FDR for his health or he would not have been there' but, the LORD revealed there are several hot springs located in Virginia, very close to the white house in DC. Plus, there are hot springs by his home in New York.

However, the deals that were made with the controlling banking families (known as 'the 12') behind the Federal Reserve by FDR were made in the "Southern White House" or "Little White House" located in Warm Springs, Georgia.

While I was in Alabama, my host family arranged a day trip to the "Little White House" and the National Park.

**Little White House**
**Warm Springs, Georgia**
**President FDR Actions Taken**

**1933. March 5. Banking Holiday. No Withdrawals allowed.**

Banks were closed for four days after inauguration March 4.

**1933. March 9.** Emergency Banking Act.

Banks were 'reorganized'; many closed, insolvent.

This Act effectively dissolved the government of America.

The nation of America was declared bankrupt and insolvent.

America was 'stolen' from the citizens through this Act.

Three days later, *Fireside Chats* began.

FDR requested all money to be put back into the banks. Nearly 75% of Americans put their money back in the banks. Gold and currency control was taken away from our representatives and handed over to the private entity, the banking families of the Federal Reserve.

**1933. April 5.** President Franklin D Roosevelt signed Executive Order **6102** which required all citizens to deliver all gold coins, gold bullion, and gold certificates to their local Federal Reserve Bank on or before April 28, 1933.

**Gold value.** During the prior 100 years gold standard held nearly even with only an increase from $18.93 to $20.69 per ounce. The Federal Reserve made the gold available to non-citizens at $35.00 per ounce. **2013 update:** President Obama signed the same Executive Order immediately after he was inaugurated. Since this action required Congress to pass the law on gold hoarding, the wording was included within the Health Reform legislation passed into law by Congress.

**1933. June 5.** Congress enacted HJR 192. This action by Congress resulted in all debts made payable by Federal Reserve backed fiat notes.

**1935. August 14.** President FDR under his **New Deal** package established the social welfare structure. Employers and employees were both required to contribute to a government fund which is identified as the **Social Security Act.**

**1937 Roosevelt** considered Wilson his mentor. He proceeded upon a plan as America being a global power. He generally ignored Hoover's concerns about the international influences already affecting the American financial structure. Wilson & Roosevelt were credited with taking America to global nation status.

Roosevelt approved supplying Britain, the Soviet Union, and China with war material through his new **Lend Lease Act.**

Sanctions were placed on Japan to supposedly deter military aggression in Asia. Truth: Japan was already at war with China. Japan's outrage resulted in the attack on Pearl Harbor.

**FDR Photo Opportunity**

As you can tell by the polished appearance of the brass statue and the seating area, it has become quite popular for tourists to pose for a photo with FDR within the national park.

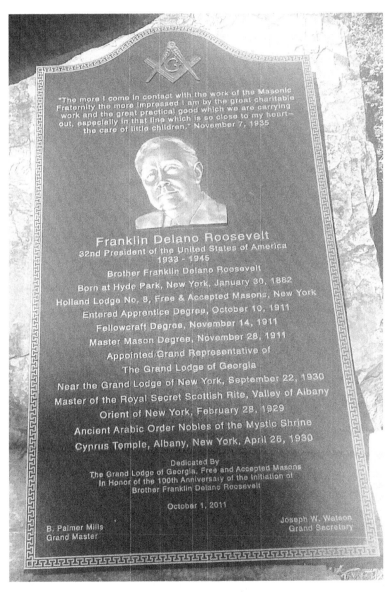

**President FDR was a 33ʳᵈ degree Mason**

**Progressive Movement Changed America.**

**President Wilson from 1913-1921.**

**President Roosevelt (FDR) 1933-1945.**

**Progressives.**

This is why historians confirm the passage of progressive legislation which changed the fundamental structure of the Republic form of government under **Wilson** was unparalleled until the extensive passage of progressive legislation by Roosevelt. Wilson began the process of the transition to a Democracy and declared it was the global goal!

President Roosevelt 'sealed the fate' of America by confirming the nation as a Democracy with majority rule and the majority having the rights vs. citizens retaining their individual sovereign rights as confirmed in the founding documents of America.

In addition to the **Agricultural Adjustment Act**, the **Tennessee Valley Authority Act**, and the **National Industrial Recovery Act**, **Roosevelt** won passage of **12 other major laws** including the **Glass-Steagall Banking Bill** and the **Home Owners' Loan Act**, within his first 100 days in office.

If one can put into place so much that affects so many lives while being influenced by the enemy to operate against America and the future for all Americans, can you imagine what one man or woman of God can accomplish since the truth is in the scriptures:

**I John 4:4. ...** *He who is in <u>you</u> is greater than he who is in the world.*

A mighty price has been paid by millions of Americans to do all we thought we knew how to do to secure our liberty and freedom.

We were 'raised' to trust! We were not aware of the enemy being entrenched within the nation, adding new laws, changing the constitution to the point of unraveling the very fabric of America!

Praying with you for us to come together, for all believers to unite in one accord, to repent for the roots revealed, to turn from our wicked ways which are revealed by the LORD and then, praying for the truth to flow from coast to coast. Then we shall hear from heaven, see the restoration of our lives, our families, our communities, our States and all across America!

**Gold is not the goal and it was never the goal.**

Many organizations are contacting Christians to transfer all of their assets into gold due to the pending currency collapse of the United States dollar. Now that you know the truth, the government plans to confiscate all of the gold, again, I trust you will not participate in the fear based plan to convert all assets into gold. Trust in God's currency, not the currency of the nation!

## HUMOR.

It reminds me of the man who was informed by an angel that he would be going to heaven that night. He raced to withdraw all funds from his bank, retirement and stock accounts. After he returned home, he wondered if the national currency would be the same currency in heaven.

He quickly decided to convert all of the currency into gold bricks. The bricks were heavy even after he packed half of the gold into each of the two suitcases. He held each of the handles with a tight grip while he waited for the angel to take him to heaven.

When he reached the pearly gates, he asked Saint Peter to set up a private meeting with God. Peter tried to convince the man it was not going to be easy to pull God away from His schedule to meet but, the man still insisted so Peter let him remain in the waiting area until the LORD had a moment to meet with him.

When the LORD entered the room, the man was excited to hand Him both suitcases. As soon as the cases were opened the LORD said, *Pavement, you brought me more pavement?*

## Chapter 21  The LORD's Promise: For The Sake Of America

The LORD confirmed to key prophets that two huge portals are positioned over Macon, Georgia and Moravian Falls, North Carolina *For The Sake Of America.*

**Moravian Falls, Prayer Mountain portal is wide open.**

**Psalm 24:7.**

Lift up your heads, O you gates!

And be lifted up, you everlasting doors!

And the King of glory shall come in.

The LORD showed each of the prophets a vision of the huge angelic vortex, a portal open to heaven over the two regions.

Moravian Falls portal was researched by the prophets. When people heard about the vision, many Christian families moved to the region. It is evident the portal over Moravian Falls is open!

The flow we experienced along with the immediate answers to prayer while we were at Prayer Mountain resulted in numerous testimonies! Friends who were not aware of our prayers testified to us the specific changes they experienced and timing confirmed the exact moments of our prayers while we were on Prayer Mountain.

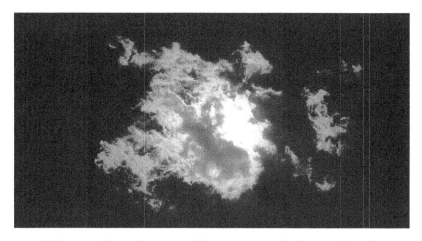

**Macon, Georgia portal is not open. It is restricted.**

Photos represent the same time of day, about 2:30 PM Eastern time, with both locations having similar cloud formations. Only a couple of light, white cumulus clouds were in the beautiful light blue sky at both locations when the photos were taken.

While we were at the top of the Ocmulgee Mounds in Macon, Georgia, the LORD clearly requested the photo. I was not going to take the photo because the sky looked exactly the same as it did when I was in Moravian Falls, North Carolina.

However, the LORD confirmed He would show me how the sky looks from His perspective and it would reveal the status of the portal, the opening to heaven over Macon, Georgia.

It was a complete surprise to see the difference in the photos taken in Macon. The photos were taken by two separate cameras and the results were absolutely identical for both cameras.

**Resurrection Power.**

**Romans 8:10-11.**

*And if Christ is in you, the body is dead because of sin, but the Spirit is life because of righteousness.*

**11** *But if the Spirit of . Him who raised Jesus from the dead dwells in you, He who raised Christ from the dead will also give life to your mortal bodies through His Spirit who dwells in you.*

Christ resides in us!

We have <u>resurrection power</u>!

Prophet Nancy Haney, co-founder of Point to Hope Ministries in Alaska shared a mighty testimony the first night I met her in January 2015. She experienced a severe stroke. The doctors were not filled with hope. They were not thinking Nancy would experience a good future after many months of rehabilitation.

Nancy is strong in her faith. She would not accept their reports. She refused to accept months of therapy and rehabilitation just for her to be able to talk and eat, or even to walk again.

As soon as the doctors left her hospital room, Nancy was determined to get up and walk!

She exerted all effort to get out of the hospital bed but, the result put her on the floor without a way to move anything.

Several employees helped Nancy get back into the hospital bed.

Nancy repented to the LORD. She gave her healing timing back to Him and in that moment, she felt a lightning bolt of power strike her body. It was so strong, her entire body lifted up off the bed for a while. She was so shocked. Without realizing it, she spoke perfectly when she asked what just happened!

The LORD confirmed Nancy was healed.

She was resurrected with His resurrection power.

Nancy's resurrection was on the third day after the stroke!

Immediately, the LORD prompted Nancy to go to Niagara Falls. As you know, Niagara Falls is a good distance from Alaska!

When they arrived, the crowd was overwhelming! Nancy told her husband she had to get out of the car at an exact spot. He was concerned due to no parking nearby but, Nancy was insistent! She told him she would be at that exact spot when he found a parking place.

The LORD directed the entire plan: The trip to New York, and the exact spot where He wanted Nancy to get out of the car.

Nancy's husband had to drive a long distance to find a place to park the car while the LORD shared a powerful word with Nancy.

Nancy stood by the railing and waited for the LORD to speak.

He asked Nancy what she noticed. At first, she said the view was beautiful. The LORD kept asking and Nancy talked about the water and how it flows from a river and into a river, etc. The LORD was waiting to make His point with Nancy about the power of the three falls which make up Niagara Falls. When she said POWER, the LORD confirmed, *There is more resurrection power within each believer than Niagara Falls!*

Wow.

My curiosity about the power of Niagara Falls immediately sent me into research mode! I've heard the sound within audio tapes of the falls while people insist it is far more significant 'in person'. The magnitude of the power generated by the falls is staggering: 4.9 million kilowatts (2.7 in America; 2.2 in the two falls in Canada). It is enough power to supply 3.8 million homes!

We have MORE power in us than in Niagara Falls! Wow!

LORD help us realize who we are in Christ!

We have hope. We have a future!

**Jeremiah 29:11.** *For I know the thoughts that I think toward you, says the LORD, thoughts of peace and not of evil, to give you a future and a hope.*

May we realize each day that we are filled with Your resurrection power for your word confirms we are more than conquerors, we are the head and not the tail, and what You have planned for us is a future and a hope!

Armed with ALL the LORD has imparted to us and in us, I pray we will take the steps to stand firm 'in truth' and pray in the seven fold return of ALL the enemy has stolen from us for it is ONLY the enemy who comes to steal, kill and destroy!


### Return Seven Times! The Promise!

The seven-fold promise is in **Proverbs 6:30-31.**

> *People* do not despise a thief
> If he steals to satisfy himself when he is starving.
> 31 Yet *when* he is found, he must restore seven-fold;
> He may have to give up all the substance of his house.

**Steps for us to take:**

**Repentance.**

Once we know what has taken place to separate us from the LORD it is important to repent so restoration can take place.

Most important question for us as members of the Body of Christ: *Will we wake up in time?*

Praying and trusting we will proceed according to the LORD's request in **II Chronicles 7:14**. *if My people who are called by My name will humble themselves, and pray and seek My face, and turn from their wicked ways, then I will hear from heaven, and will forgive their sin and heal their land.*

Many think the land is the earth of a nation, of America.

Personally, I trust since we came from the dust we are the 'hunk of dust' the LORD is referring to as the land.

Are we willing to take individual responsibility?

America has become a Sodom and Gomorrah.

People challenge me when I share this statement since they think Sodom and Gomorrah was all about sex and lust. That is not the truth or the whole story!

The people aligned with the world. They separated themselves from God. They became comfortable. Their needs were met by their own labors. Since they trusted their knowledge and their understanding that 'me and mine are fine' they clearly did not see they were actually protected by the LORD in spite of themselves.

**Bottom line:** Lot could not convince ten to repent, humble themselves and turn from their wicked ways to save the region!

In fact, Lot could not even convince his two son-in-laws! The husbands of his daughters would not leave with Lot. His son-in-laws were destroyed with all of the other residents because they would not leave with Lot when the angel offered time for Lot to speak with them and bring them to the gate.

**Lot waited at the gate for the LORD.**

**Proverbs 8:34. Amplified Bible.** *Blessed* [happy, prosperous, to be admired] *is the man who listens to me, watching daily at my gates, waiting at my doorposts*.

Will we wait?

Will we humble ourselves, turn from our wicked ways, and wait upon the LORD at the gate?

Will we seek His truth in these days and align with His purpose and plan for us, our families, and our nation?

Or, will we allow ourselves to be separated from the LORD and His promise thinking 'me and mine are fine' instead of knowing for sure that me and my house serve the only living LORD?

**Genesis 19:1-22. Amplified Bible, The Doom of Sodom**

It was evening when the two angels came to Sodom. Lot was sitting at Sodom's [city] gate. Seeing them, Lot got up to meet them and bowed down *with his* face to the ground.

² And he said, *"See here, my lords, please turn aside and come into your servant's house, and spend the night, and wash your feet; then you may get up early and go on your way."* But they said, **"No, we shall spend the night in the open plaza** [of the city]*.*"

³ However, Lot strongly urged them, so they turned aside and entered his house; and he prepared a feast for them [with wine], and baked unleavened bread, and they ate.

⁴ But before they lay down [to sleep], the men of the city, the men of Sodom, both young and old, surrounded the house, all the men from every quarter; ⁵ and they called out to Lot and said to him, **"Where are the men who came to you tonight? Bring them out to us so that we may know them** [intimately]**."**

⁶ But Lot went out of the doorway to the men, and shut the door after him, ⁷ and said, **"Please, my brothers, do not do something so wicked.**

⁸ *See here, I have two daughters who have not known a man* [intimately]; *please let me bring them out to you* [instead], *and you can do as you please with them; only do nothing to these men, because they have in fact come under the shelter of my roof* [for protection]*."*

⁹ But they said, *"Get out of the way!"* And they said, *"This man (Lot) came* [as an outsider] *to live here temporarily, and now he is acting like a judge. Now we will treat you worse than your*

*visitors!*" So they rushed forward *and* pressed violently against Lot and came close to breaking down the door [of his house].

10 But the men (angels) reached out with their hands and pulled Lot into the house with them, and shut the door [after him].

11 They struck (punished) the men who were at the doorway of the house with blindness, from the young men to the old men, so that they exhausted *themselves trying* to find the doorway.

12 And the [two] men (angels) asked Lot, *"Have you any others here* [in Sodom]—*a son-in-law, and your sons, and your daughters? Whomever you have in the city, take them out of here;* 13 *for we are destroying this place, because the outcry* [for judgment] *against them has grown so great before the LORD that the LORD has sent us to destroy and ruin it."*

14 So Lot went out and spoke to his sons-in-law, who were [betrothed, and legally promised] to marry his daughters, and said, *"Get up, get out of this place, for the LORD is about to destroy this city!"* But to his sons-in-law he appeared to be joking.

15 When morning dawned, the angels urged Lot [to hurry], saying, *"Get up! Take your wife and two daughters who are here* [and go], *or you will be swept away in the punishment of the city."*

16 But Lot hesitated *and* lingered. The men took hold of his hand and the hand of his wife and the hands of his two daughters, because the LORD was merciful to him [for Abraham's sake]; and

they brought him out, and left him outside the city [with his family].

<sup>17</sup> When they had brought them outside, one [of the angels] said, *"Escape for your life! Do not look behind you, or stop anywhere in the entire valley; escape to the mountains* [of Moab], *or you will be consumed and swept away."*

<sup>18</sup> But Lot said to them, *"Oh no,* [not that place] *my lords!*

<sup>19</sup> *Please listen, your servant has found favor in your sight, and you have magnified your loving kindness (mercy) to me by saving my life; but I cannot escape to the mountains, because the disaster will overtake me and I will be killed.*

<sup>20</sup> *Now look, this town* [in the distance] *is near enough for us to flee to, and it is small* [with only a few people]. *Please, let me escape there* (is it not small?) *so that my life will be saved."*

<sup>21</sup> And the angel said to him, *"Behold, I grant you this request also; I will not destroy this town of which you have spoken.*

<sup>22</sup> *Hurry and take refuge there, for I cannot do anything* [to punish Sodom] *until you arrive there."* For this reason the town was named Zoar (few, small).

Will we wait and seek the promise of the LORD for America?

Will the angels find us separate from the world, waiting and ready?

**Daniel waited.**

**Daniel 10:13.** *But the prince of the kingdom of Persia withstood me twenty-one days; and behold, Michael, one of the chief princes* (Archangel, the prince angel), **came to help me, for I had been left alone there with the kings of Persia.**


**Elijah followed instructions and waited.**

**I Kings 19:9-18. Amplified Bible.**

**Elijah at Horeb**

There he came to a cave and spent the night in it; and behold, the word of the Lord *came* to him, and He said to him, *"What are you doing here, Elijah?"*

**10** He said, *"I have been very zealous* (impassioned) *for the Lord God of hosts* (armies) [proclaiming what is rightfully and uniquely His]; *for the sons of Israel have abandoned* (broken) *Your covenant, torn down Your altars, and killed Your prophets with the sword. And I, only I, am left; and they seek to take away my life."*

**11** So He said, *"Go out and stand on the mountain before the Lord."* And behold, the Lord was passing by, and a great and powerful wind was tearing out the mountains and breaking the rocks in pieces before the Lord; but the Lord was not in the wind. And after the wind, [there was] an earthquake, but the Lord was not in the earthquake.

**12** After the earthquake, [there was] a fire, but the Lord was not in the fire; and after the fire, [there was] the sound of a gentle blowing.

**13** When Elijah heard *the sound*, he wrapped his face in his mantle (cloak) and went out and stood in the entrance of the cave. And behold, a voice came to him and said, ***"What are you doing here, Elijah?"***

**14** He said, ***"I have been very zealous for the Lord God of hosts*** (armies), ***because the sons of Israel have abandoned*** (broken) ***Your covenant, torn down Your altars and killed Your prophets with the sword. And I, only I, am left; and they seek to take away my life."***

**15** The Lord [d]said to him, ***"Go, return on your way to the Wilderness of Damascus; and when you arrive, you shall anoint Hazael as king over Aram*** (Syria); **16** *and you shall anoint Jehu the son of Nimshi as king over Israel; and anoint Elisha the son of Shaphat of Abel-meholah as prophet in your place.*

**17** *It shall come about that Jehu shall put to death whoever escapes from the sword of Hazael, and Elisha shall put to death whoever escapes the sword of Jehu.*

**18** ***Yet I will leave 7,000 [survivors] in Israel, all the knees that have not bowed down to Baal and every mouth that has not kissed him."***

Will we be among the few?

Will we become the people in America who have not participated with the pagan gods?

Will we be able to say we have not bowed to Baal?

Will we stop gathering with those who worship Ishtar and proceed with her Easter fertility rituals which are represented as bunny eggs died with food coloring as the representation of the blood of babies produced for the rituals within pagan worship?

With truth 'in hand' will we be bold enough to ask the pastors to not hide eggs or become competitive to see if the church can hide the most eggs in the region on the pagan worship day of Easter?

Will we adjust to the truth?

Will we only honor the true death and resurrection of Christ?

Will we adjust to the truth?

Will we only honor the true birth of Christ?

Will we adjust to the truth?

Will we stop worship of the sun god Baal on December 25?

Will we adjust to the truth?

Will we return to the true Hebrew calendar and Jewish feasts and festivals? Will we honor the truth? The birth of Christ is recognized as the first day of the Feast of Tabernacles.

With the truth 'in hand' that the Jewish people journeyed to Jerusalem for the Feast of Tabernacles, the time when the taxes were submitted due to all of the people gathering together for the Feast days, will we proceed upon the truth or follow the pagan worship called Christmas which has become 'tradition'?

### Jacob saw the portal to heaven.

When Jacob saw the portal to heaven open above, he trusted he was having a dream. However, when we see the full scripture it is clear the LORD personally appeared to Jacob in an open vision.

### Genesis 28:10-22. Amplified Bible. Jacob's Dream.

Now Jacob left Beersheba [never to see his mother again] and traveled toward Haran.

11And he came to a certain place and stayed overnight there because the sun had set. Taking one of the stones of the place, he put it under his head and lay down there [to sleep].

12 He dreamed that there was a ladder (stairway) placed on the earth, and the top of it reached [out of sight] toward heaven; and [he saw] the angels of God ascending and descending on it [going to and from heaven].

13 And behold, the Lord stood above *and* around him and said, "I am the Lord, the God of Abraham your [father's] father and the God of Isaac; I will give to you and to your descendants the land [of promise] on which you are lying.

**14** Your descendants shall be as [countless as] the dust of the earth, and you shall spread abroad to the west and the east and the north and the south; and all the families (nations) of the earth shall be blessed through you and your[c]descendants.

**15** Behold, I am with you and will keep [careful watch over you and guard] you wherever you may go, and I will bring you back to this [promised] land; for I will not leave you until I have done what I have promised you.

**16** Then Jacob awoke from his sleep and he said, *"Without any doubt the Lord is in this place, and I did not realize it."*

**17** So he was afraid and said, *"How fearful and awesome is this place! This is none other than the house of God, and this is the gateway to heaven."*

**18** So Jacob got up early in the morning, and took the stone he had put under his head and he set it up as a pillar [that is, a monument to the vision in his dream], and he poured [olive] oil on the top of it [to consecrate it].

**19** He named that place Bethel (the house of God); the previous name of that city was Luz (Almond Tree).

**20** Then Jacob made a vow (promise), saying, *"If God will be with me and will keep me on this journey that I take, and will give me food to eat and clothing to wear,* **21** *and if* [He grants that] *I return to my father's house in safety, then the Lord will be my God.*

**22** *This stone which I have set up as a pillar* (monument, memorial) *will be God's house* [a sacred place to me], *and of everything that You give me I will give the tenth to You* [as an offering to signify my gratitude and dependence on You]. "

## Stone(s) of Remembrance

Exactly as the '12 stones of remembrance' are positioned where the Israelites crossed the Jordan so all future generations would hear the truth and remember what the LORD had done for the people who remained aligned with the LORD, Jacob placed the stone where he rested and received the message from the LORD as a place of remembrance.

## Monuments in America

In America, we have erected monuments and honored individual men who clearly operated against the people and the word of God. A few examples are shared within these pages.

## What Can We Do?

**II Chronicles 7:14**. *if My people who are called by My name will humble themselves, and pray and seek My face, and turn from their wicked ways, then I will hear from heaven, and will forgive their sin and heal their land.*

1. Gain a close relationship with the LORD, today!

   Seek His truth! Align with His will! Speak His truth!

   Knowing He never leaves or forsakes us.

   Knowing we are more than conquerors.

   Knowing we are the head and not the tail.

   Knowing who we represent when we walk in faith.

2. Humble ourselves.

3. Pray.

4. Seek the LORD in all things.

5. Repent of free will and align with the LORD's will.

6. Turn from our wicked ways.

7. Wait upon the LORD. Repent and align with His will!

8. Listen for His voice; receive confirmation from Him.

9. Unite together with members of the body of Christ.

   Share the truth with whosoever will come to hear truth!

   Pray repentance prayers with each one; restoring life.

10. He will honor your prayers.

11. He will forgive your sins.

12. He will heal you, your land, each community & nation!

We are responsible!

We cannot blame the Government, Congress or the Media!

Within the Declaration of Independence, **We The People** have the opportunity and the responsibility to counter the actions of the government.

> *We hold these truths to be self-evident, that all men are created equal, that they are endowed by their Creator with certain unalienable Rights, that among these are Life, Liberty and the pursuit of Happiness.--That to secure these rights, Governments are instituted among Men, deriving their just powers from the consent of the governed, --That whenever any Form of Government becomes destructive of these ends, it is the Right of the People to alter or to abolish it, and to institute new Government, laying its foundation on such principles and organizing its powers in such form, as to them shall seem most likely to effect their Safety and Happiness.*

### Next Step: PRAY FOR AND LOVE YOUR ENEMIES!

**Matthew 5:43-45.** *"You have heard that it was said, 'You shall love your neighbor and hate your enemy.'*

*44 But I say to you, love your enemies, bless those who curse you, do good to those who hate you, and pray for those who spitefully use you and persecute you, 45 that you may be sons of your Father in heaven; for He makes His sun rise on the evil and on the good, and sends rain on the just and on the unjust.*

### Next Step: Communicate Truth to ALL in Leadership!

Be in communication with State and National representatives. Request the return to, the restoration of America!

### Next Step: Communicate Truth to ALL in Your Region!

Continue to invest daily time with fellow believers and non-believers to pass on the truth to all who have ears to hear and eyes to see! Remember, Christ remained with the people in the region. He did not limit himself to those who 'already knew the truth'. He demonstrated the truth! We are to do the same and more!

We often hear **1 Corinthians 2:9 that eye has not seen nor ear heard nor can the mind conceive what the LORD has 'in store' for those who love Him** but, the value is in the entire message since it reveals the depth of the words for us to capture the full meaning of verse 9. Plus, it explains why the LORD sent me to Georgia, not as a powerful woman in the world only as a servant willing to serve. **1 Corinthians 2:1-16. Amplified. Paul's Reliance upon the Spirit.** And when I came to you, brothers and sisters, proclaiming to you the testimony of God [concerning salvation through Christ], I did not come with superiority of speech or of wisdom [no lofty words of eloquence or of philosophy as a Greek orator might do]; **2** for I made the decision to know nothing [that is, to forego philosophical or theological discussions regarding inconsequential things and opinions while] among you except Jesus Christ, and Him crucified [and the meaning of His redemptive, substitutionary death and His resurrection].

**3** I came to you in weakness and fear and great trembling.

**4** And my message and my preaching were not in persuasive words of wisdom [using clever rhetoric], but [they were delivered] in demonstration of the [Holy] Spirit [operating through me] and of [His] power [stirring the minds of the listeners and persuading them], **5** so that your faith would not rest on the wisdom *and* rhetoric of men, but on the power of God.

**6** Yet we do speak wisdom among those *spiritually* mature [believers who have teachable hearts and a greater understanding]; but [it is a higher] wisdom not [the wisdom] of this *present* age nor of the rulers *and* leaders of this age, who are passing away; **7** but we speak God's wisdom in a mystery, the *wisdom* once hidden [from man, but now revealed to us by God, that wisdom] which God predestined before the ages to our glory [to lift us into the glory of His presence].

**8** None of the rulers of this age recognized *and* understood this *wisdom*; for if they had, they would not have crucified the Lord of glory **9** but just as it is written [in Scripture], ***"Things which the eye has not seen and the ear has not heard, and which have not entered the heart of man, all that God has prepared for those who love Him*** [who hold Him in affectionate reverence, who obey Him, and who gratefully recognize the benefits that He has bestowed]."

**10** For God has unveiled them *and* revealed *them* to us through the [Holy] Spirit; for the Spirit searches all things [diligently], even [sounding and measuring] the [profound] depths of God [the divine counsels and things far beyond human understanding].

**11** For what person knows the thoughts and motives of a man except the man's spirit within him? So also no one knows the *thoughts* of God except the Spirit of God.

**12** Now we have received, not the spirit of the world, but the [Holy] Spirit who is from God, so that we may know *and* understand the [wonderful] things freely given to us by God.

**13** We also speak of these things, not in words taught *or* supplied by human wisdom, but in those taught by the Spirit, combining *and* interpreting spiritual *thoughts* with spiritual *words* [for those being guided by the Holy Spirit].

**14** But the natural [unbelieving] man does not accept the things [the teachings and revelations] of the Spirit of God, for they are foolishness [absurd and illogical] to him; and he is incapable of understanding them, because they are spiritually discerned *and* appreciated, [and he is unqualified to judge spiritual matters].

**15** But the spiritual man [the spiritually mature Christian] judges all things [questions, examines and applies what the Holy Spirit reveals], yet is himself judged by no one [the unbeliever cannot judge and understand the believer's spiritual nature].

**16** For who has known the mind *and* purposes of the Lord, so as to instruct Him? But we have the mind of Christ [to be guided by His thoughts and purposes].

So now you know the initial steps to take.

You also know it is absolutely not about me or that the LORD chose to send me to Georgia out of the entire nation of believers!

The LORD has kept it simple.

He sent a woman to Georgia with one suitcase and a lap top.

He revealed His truth about the actual history of our nation, especially from Macon, Georgia to Moravian Falls, North Carolina. Due to all that was put in place for the north half of the LORD's plan (Mountains of Georgia to Moravian Falls, North Carolina) we already see evidence! The LORD has promised a way for us to live, to worship and pray together to redeem our lives, to restore the years and the land! Will you join in repentance prayer?

Macon to the 'mountaintop' is the south half which needs work!

Now that the truth is revealed to you, I pray we will come together, willing to participants in repenting for all that was done against the people and the land so we will live in truth, speak truth, regain the blessings upon our lives, our families, our communities and the blessed ONE NATION UNDER GOD known as America!

I pray we will be willing to repent for all our LORD brings to mind. Then, pray through and do what we can do to correct the errors and help each of us in our daily lives, our families and our America to heal and prosper once again as our souls prosper!

Pray from your position within the body of Christ no matter where the LORD has placed your feet upon the soil!

The atrocities in Georgia and the Carolinas are examples which reveal the roots which require repentance prayers and action steps made known by the LORD, to work with the LORD in turning it all around for the sake of the current and future generations.

Individually as believers and members of the body of Christ, remember, we each have resurrection power and authority and that multiplies again when two or more gather together for then our Christ is in the midst with us!

**Matthew 18:19-20. Amplified.** *"Again I say to you, that if two believers on earth agree*[that is, are of one mind, in harmony] *about anything that they ask* [within the will of God], *it will be done for them by My Father in heaven.*

**20** *For where two or three are gathered in My name* [meeting together as My followers], *I am there among them."*

When we gather together, repent, seek the LORD's truth, and turn from our wicked human ways, then He will hear our cries from heaven. Angels will be dispatched from heaven which will also expand the portal so the flow will return in our life as it did for Daniel, Jacob, and Elijah. Then, it will expand over the region, across the State of Georgia and flood across the nation of America for the LORD promises the truth will spread from Georgia across the nation of America like a mighty flood!

This is exactly what the LORD promised in the vision He shared with the prophets before they went to Heaven: Bob Jones, February 2014, Arthur Burt, August 2014, and John Paul Jackson, February 2015.

Do we have anything else we need to do?

Yes.

Strengthen our faith and our belief and give credit to the only living LORD over our lives who grants us hope and a future!

Where we are weak, He is strong!

**II Corinthians 13:7-9.**

Now I pray to God that you do no evil, not that we should appear approved, but that you should do what is honorable, though we may seem disqualified.

**8** For we can do nothing against the truth, but for the truth.

**9** For we are glad when we are weak and you are strong. And this also we pray, that you may be made complete.

It's NOT me LORD, it's all about You LORD!

**II Corinthians 12:7-10.** And lest I should be exalted above measure by the abundance of the revelations, a thorn in the flesh was given to me, a messenger of Satan to buffet me, lest I be exalted above measure **8** Concerning this thing I pleaded with the Lord three times that it might depart from me.**9** And He said to me, ***"My grace is sufficient for you, for My strength is made perfect in weakness."*** Therefore most gladly I will rather boast in my infirmities, that the power of Christ may rest upon me.

**10** Therefore I take pleasure in infirmities, in reproaches, in needs, in persecutions, in distresses, for Christ's sake. For when I am weak, then I am strong.

The LORD's promise depends entirely on faith so that the promise will be (legally) guaranteed to us as joint heirs with Christ for we are in the line of Abraham.

Then, we are to pass on the truth, the word, to all of the generations!

**Romans 4:16-25. Amplified Bible.** Therefore, [inheriting] the promise depends entirely on faith [that is, confident trust in the unseen God], in order that *it may be given* as an act of grace [His unmerited favor and mercy], so that the promise will be [legally] guaranteed to all the descendants [of Abraham]—not only for those [Jewish believers] who keep the Law, but also for those [Gentile believers] who share the faith of Abraham, who is the [spiritual] father of us all— **17** (as it is written [in Scripture], "I have made you a father of many nations") in the sight of Him in whom he believed, that is, God who gives life to the dead and calls into being that which does not exist.

**18** In hope against hope Abraham believed that he would become a father of many nations, as he had been promised [by God]: "So [numberless] shall your descendants be."

**19** Without becoming weak in faith he considered his own body, now as good as dead [for producing children] since he was about a hundred years old, and [he considered] the deadness of Sarah's womb.

**20** But he did not doubt *or* waver in unbelief concerning the promise of God, but he grew strong *and* empowered by faith, giving glory to God, **21** being fully convinced that God had the power to do what He had promised.

**22** Therefore his faith was credited to him as righteousness (right standing with God).

**23** Now not for his sake alone was it written that it was credited to him, **24** but for our sake also—to whom righteousness will be credited, as those who believe in Him who raised Jesus our Lord from the dead— **25** who was betrayed *and* crucified because of our sins, and was raised [from the dead] because of our justification [our acquittal—absolving us of all sin before God].

### Hope For America

Crying out to the LORD to know if there are more visions and words which align with His plans for America.

He prompted me to review the words and visions of many prophets in many nations who have stated similar words and shared the same visions. They are saying what the LORD did with Cyrus is what He will do with a candidate for Presdient in 2016 *For The Sake of America* as the LORD did for Persia. Interesting the position America is in with Persia/Iran in these days! Prophets and scholars argue whether or not 'Cyrus was anointed'. However, it is clearly stated in **Isaiah 45:1** whether you are doing research in King James, New King James or Amplified, etc., the LORD calls Cyrus His anointed.

**Isaiah 45:1-** .This is what the Lord says to His anointed, *to Cyrus* [king of Persia], *whose right hand I have held to subdue nations before him, and I will ungird the loins of kings* [disarming them]; *to open doors before him so that gates will not be shut:* 2 *"I will go before you and level the mountains; I will shatter the doors of bronze and cut through the bars of iron.* 3 *"I will give you the treasures of darkness* [the hoarded treasures] *and the hidden riches of secret places, so that you may know that it is I, The Lord, the God of Israel, who calls you* (Cyrus the Great) *by your name.*

Key visions align with the word:

1. Daystar production crew received a vision in 2012 before the election. John Paul Jackson interpreted the bulldozer the LORD was sending before the election of 2016 as a sign the LORD was going to reveal much to the believers. The LORD knew a bulldozer

would be required for the 'behind the scenes actions to be made known to the believers. This is available on You Tube.

2. Mark Taylor received a word about the LORD's hand being upon America through this time and during the 'Reconstruction of America'.

3. Stephen Powell, Lion of Light Ministries, Fort Mill, South Carolina was given a vision (Angelic Visitation from a Presidential Guardian) and word from the LORD. It aligns with both topics: 1. Cyrus anointing, 2. Financial turn around (once the roots are repented for and restoration is evident) *For The Sake of America!*

**LORD thank you for your promise!**

**Thank You for revealing what we need to do to prepare to march before the SONrise!**

**We are your Army on the Earth. We must pray and repent for the roots so the portal You have positioned over Macon, Georgia will open wide!**

**Thank You for providing the angelic vortexes over Macon, Georgia and Moravian Falls, North Carolina *'For The Sake Of America'!***

Thank you for providing Your truth in Your word and through Your prophets so we will be prepared to march with You before the SONrise!

Grateful to know Your hand is upon us and You will never leave us or forsake us!

# Research

## Three Years in Georgia, After Training and Equipping by the LORD For These Days in Georgia!

1. **Gary Kah** documents on **Lucis Trust, Illuminati & The Masonic Order in America; Dr. David Reagan** on **Georgia Guidestones,** link to **Lucis Trust;** *The Hidden Dangers of the Rainbow* by **Constance Cumby.**

2. **Lucis Trust within Illuminati, United Nations, One World Order, World Goodwill, Lifebridge Foundation, Trust for Conservation, and New Group of World Servers; Foundation(s) involved within New Group World Servers; Spiritual Caucus at the United Nations; research by Christian Voice UK.**

3. **Dr. John Benefiel** and *Binding The Strongman Over America* (Baal).

4. **Benjamin Hawkins** biography.

5. **Creek Muskogean** history of largest tribe north of Mexico.

6. **Georgia, South & North Carolina,** and **Alabama** history.

7. **William Wyatt Bibb** and **John Birch** biography.

8. **Petersburg, Georgia; Elberton, Georgia** history.

9. **Albert Pike** biography; **Civil War & Confederate States, Macon arsenal & planned Confederate Capital** history.

10. **President Woodrow Wilson** biography and **Ambassador to Mexico, Henry Lane Wilson** biography.

11. **Supreme Court Justice Joseph Lamar** biography.

12. **President Franklin D Roosevelt** (FDR) biography.

## Personal Note 'Just Between Us'

What the LORD does through us may not 'make sense' to the people who seek man's approval vs. the LORD's approval. Whether the message is popular or not, or it makes us popular or not, it does not matter since lives are at stake!

In the book of **Numbers, Chapter 13,** the LORD spoke to Moses. He requested of Moses to send the leaders of the 12 tribes to 'check on the land promised to Israel'.

Only two, Joshua and Caleb, saw the land as the promise, the opportunity for their future. Ten of the leaders spoke against the plan. The ten focused on every problem they saw while they were 'on the land'. The ten leaders were showing the people they were closely aligned together 'in their human understanding' and the people immediately became upset and aligned with the ten.

Then, one leader stood firm and quieted the crowd. His name was Caleb. He spoke the truth to the people in **Numbers 13:30b.** *"Let us go up at once and take possession, for we are well able to overcome it."*

As we know now, one person can make a huge difference!

Are you one who will stand firm and make a difference?

Or will you and your family follow the 'human understanding' when someone gathers a group together and their words 'sound good'.

We must discern the LORD's truth all of our days and especially in these days for this is a critical time in our history. All of the roots from long ago have grown into a huge 'human thing' which we have allowed for too many decades.

We have the opportunity to quiet the current storm of negative conversation in our nation by 'being a Caleb' and sharing the truth, helping all to repent, align with the LORD to bring the truth to all who have ears to hear and eyes to see. We are the majority of the people within this nation and we can turn the tide in America!

America is our promised land!

We have the right to change what is not working in the government. That right is clearly described within the beginning of our American Declaration of Independence:

*We hold these truths to be self-evident, that all men are created equal, that they are endowed by their Creator with* *certain unalienable Rights, that among these are Life, Liberty and the pursuit of Happiness.--That <u>to secure these rights, Governments are instituted among Men, deriving their just powers from the consent of the governed, --That whenever any Form of Government becomes destructive of these ends, it is the Right of the People to alter or to abolish it, and to institute new Government, laying its foundation on such principles and organizing its powers in such form, as to them shall seem most likely to effect their Safety and Happiness.</u>*

The question for each American to consider remains:

Will you become one of the 10 and align with the crowd?

Or, will you stand firm with the LORD, quiet the people unaware of the truth, and speak the truth about the opportunity to all who have ears to hear and eyes to see?

During the trials and temptations, we are to be as wise as serpents while we remain as gentle as doves.

Remember, even Jesus Christ was misunderstood, maligned, spoken about and spoken against, persecuted and crucified by the devout within the fellowship!


**Matthew 10:16-20.**

"Behold, I send you out as sheep in the midst of wolves. Therefore be wise as serpents and harmless as doves.

**17** But beware of men, for they will deliver you up to councils and scourge you in their synagogues.

**18** You will be brought before governors and kings for My sake, as a testimony to them and to the Gentiles.

**19** But when they deliver you up, do not worry about how or what you should speak. For it will be given to you in that hour what you should speak; **20** for it is not you who speak, but the Spirit of your Father who speaks in you.


America is not about a candidate and yet, a candidate has made a key point for us to work upon. Christians are the largest voting block. Until we have a voice within the process, how can we state we expect justice is to be rendered the same for all citizens 'in the world'.

Knowing all of this to be true we are NOT to speak against the people. We are to pray for them, for our leaders, and for all who are in a position of power!

Pray for America. Pray for Georgia, North & South Carolina.

Pray for all of the states in the nation. Pray for all leaders.

Pray for unity within the body of Christ, in our homes, our communities, and all States across the nation until America heals.

THANK the LORD that His hand is upon us and all plans of the enemy are thwarted, for the LORD's hand to be upon America and His favor to be evident and shared in the testimonies from ALL of the people within the Body of Christ in these days.

Remember the word is the truth and the LORD's promise is based upon our willingness to stand firm in faith!

Deep in our heart where Christ resides, we do know there is ONLY ONE WAY, ONE TRUTH, ONLY ONE NAME ABOVE ALL NAMES, ONLY ONE SAVIOR Jesus Christ of Nazareth, the ONLY Son of the Father, our LORD Almighty, the ONLY LIVING LORD.

Trusting the facts shared help us see the truth to know what to do and how to proceed to do the things Christ did and greater!

To live from glory to glory, it is important to comprehend that the Messiah gave us the glory that we would be one as He and the Father are one, while He was with us!

Yikes! We do have a lot of work to do!

The good news is the LORD is with us!

Praying and trusting that now, since you are armed with the truth and realize how powerful we are in Christ, you will be willing to pray powerfully, and with authority for your situations and issues, and the situations and issues of the people in your life, and the people the LORD sends to you!

Remember, when you walk in the truth guided by the Holy Spirit, it's easy to know what to do since the adventures laid out before you are divinely orchestrated by the LORD!

You merely have to show up!

May you take the LORD's hand and proceed with His wisdom while enjoying experiences which inspire, encourage and re-encourage you, your family, the people in your community and future generations! I look forward to hearing your testimonies!

Until the next ONE MORE TIME our Lord brings us together may you continue to experience HIS Best!

## Sheila

**Email: hisbest4usorders@gmail.com**

**Use the Subject Line: *For The Sake Of America***

**Ephesians 2:19-22** *We are no longer foreigners and aliens, but fellow citizens... members of God's household, built on the foundation of the apostles and prophets, with Christ Jesus himself as the chief cornerstone. In Him the whole building is joined together and rises to become a holy temple in the Lord. And in Him you too are being built together to become a dwelling in which God lives by His Spirit.*

**II Corinthians 12:14-15. (a)** *"Now, I am ready to visit you...what I want is not your possessions but you...So I will very gladly spend for you everything I have and expend myself as well."*

**II Corinthians 13:11-14.** *Aim for perfection ... be of one mind, live in peace, and the God of love and peace will be with you. May the grace of the Lord Jesus Christ, and the love of God, and the fellowship of the Holy Spirit be with you all.*

# Books Authored by Sheila Holm

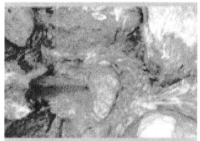

## A Wake Up Call: It's Restoration Time!

MYSTERIES REVEALED: HOW AND WHEN
THE CHURCH WAS DECEIVED AND WHAT
IS REQUIRED FOR FULL RESTORATION.

## SHEILA HOLM

## IN SEARCH OF WIGGLESWORTH

A JOURNEY WHICH SPEAKS TO THE
VERY CORE OF WHAT IT MEANS TO BE A
TRUE BROTHER AND SISTER IN CHRIST!

## SHEILA HOLM

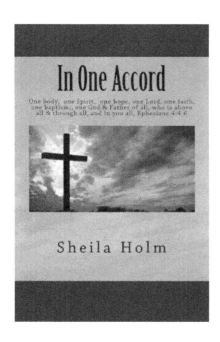

In One Accord

One body, one Spirit, one hope, one Lord, one faith,
one baptism; one God & Father of all, who is above
all & through all, and in you all. Ephesians 4:4-6

Sheila Holm

## A PECULIAR PEOPLE

A holy nation,
a peculiar people.

We are not ashamed of the Gospel of Jesus Christ!!!

DISCIPLESHIP OF PECULIAR
PEOPLE BY PECULIAR PEOPLE

## SHEILA HOLM

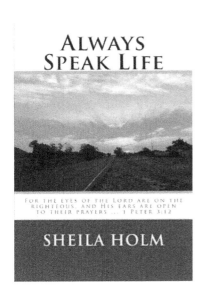

**Releasing soon ...**

**Nation Restoration**

**Published in 2014**

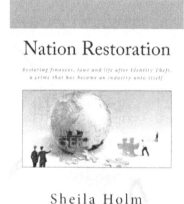

## Nation Restoration

Restoring finances, laws and life after Identity Theft,
a crime that has become an industry unto itself

Sheila Holm

**Seven Step Business Plan**

**Published, 2007**

**Latin America edition:**

**Spanish Language**

**Published, 2009**

# ACKNOWLEDGMENTS

## AFRICA

### *Ghana, West Africa*

*Pastor Sam Ankrah*

**"Truly, God has sent you to us with a  strong  word for our church."**

*Pastor Charles Benneh*

**"It blesses my soul to hear of your faith & see the fruit of the ministry."**

*Johannesburg, South Africa*

*Pastor Jhanni,*

**"God is doing a good work through you and I pray with you and our church."**

# Coronation Ceremony

## AMERICA

*Dr. Nancy Franklin, Georgia*

"Thank you God for answering my prayers by sending Your apostle to (the region) to unite the believers ... "

*Prophetess Nancy Haney, Alaska*

"God has never given me this before. I see circles and circles and circles ... you drink and you draw from one circle to the other, and that's what you do, you drink and draw and you bring these circles together ... Pulling many groups together.

All these groups need each other ... He can use you for you have ears to hear and you hear His deep truth. You are filtering what is nonsense and what is real ... because you have been in that circle, and because of what you say they are going to merge. It is going to expand, become bigger than you could imagine."

*Pastor, Host of "Praise the Lord", TBN*

"…The fruit of the ministry is evident in your testimony…"

*Man of God (Georgia), Requesting to be Discipled while attending the coronation of a King in Africa*

"…at my age, it is hard to believe I am learning so much in these few days about what I did not know…realizing what it is to know that I know how it is to live within God's word each day. Will you consider discipling me?"

*International Prophet*

"You have remained steadfast to God's plan and God will continue to send you forth for His plan and purpose to be fulfilled, and for the thousands who have not knelt…"

*President, Christian Publishing Company*

**"Only God could orchestrate such a grand plan…"**

*Prayer Director, International Prayer Center*

**"God is opening many doors for you…"**

*Christian Publisher,* **"God has given you a powerful voice and a sweet spirit…"**

*Pastor, Southern California*

**"God is raising you up and sending you forth to many nations…"**

*International Apostle*

**"God is doing a mighty work through you, for His righteousness precedes you, showers over you and follows you as a mighty wake. May it continue for each of your days…"**

*Prophetic Prayer Partner, Minnesota*

**"Only God could walk you through these days… accomplish so much through you, in the midst of your daily situations, the many blessings shared during each of your travels will continue to shower blessings upon each of the many households around the world…"**

# AUSTRALIA

*Newcastle, New South Wales, Australia*

*Pastor Mark,* "...**the staff and business leaders heard the message of Personal and Professional Life Management this week, so we are blessed you agreed to preach the word to our church this morning.**"

*Four Square Gospel Church, Aboriginal Cultural Center*
*Pastor Rex,* "**God blessed us through your preaching on Easter Sunday. We will never forget that you were in our midst ... God brought new people to Jesus today and we thank God for what He has done because you answered His call.**"

*Prayer Team Meeting* **"We know now how we will we be able to continue this mighty work when you are not in our midst…"**

## ENGLAND

### *London, England*

*Pastor Vincent, Glory House, East London,*

> **"…the honor is ours this Easter Sunday."**

*Associate Pastor,*

> **"The Glory of our God Almighty shines upon you and through you in your speaking and your actions…we give Him praise."**

*Protocol Team,*

> **"God has mightily blessed us, by sending you into our midst."**

*Pastor Arnold,*

> **"You have blessed the people of this congregation, and in His wisdom and timing, may He bring you back into our midst again, very soon."**

*Pastor, West London,*

**"We rejoice with you in hearing and   seeing   the mighty things God is doing."**

*Pastor, South London,* **"Our God is evidenced in your life and your speaking, while we continue to thank God for the work He is doing through you…"**

*High Commissioner, Kingdom of Tonga, serving in the Embassy in London, England; Ambassador Akosita,* **"God's timing is always right…for you to be with us, prior to the Economic Summit, to meet and pray with us…"**

*Anglican, Former Church of Pastor Smith Wigglesworth*

*Pastor Day,* "**I thank God for sending you to our church this morning, for serving communion to me, and for renewing and restoring me for the call upon my life.**"

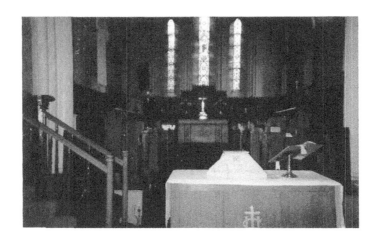

# Kingdom of TONGA

*Pastor Isileli Taukolo,* "**Our board and business leaders were fasting and praying and God confirmed He was sending someone to us. We are deeply touched by the message God sent to us, through you.**"

*Minister of Finance, Tasi,* "**Our meeting was an answer to my prayers, and I thank you for providing the seminar for our senior staff members, and meeting with them individually for prayer and coaching.**"

*Government Office,* "**Thank you for speaking today and for staying and praying with us.**"

Interpreter, Sela

## About the Author

The LORD fulfills upon His promises within the scriptures. He has equipped and trained Sheila while He:

- Places her feet on the soil of each continent,
- Sends her forth without an extra coin or tunic,
- Arranges flights and accommodations in each nation,
- Introduces her before she arrives,
- Lifts her up and encourages her,
- Seats her before governors and kings,
- Fills her as an empty vessel,
- Shares His wisdom and word of knowledge,
- Blesses and heals the people in her path,
- Comforts & re-encourages her to encourage pastors, prophets, apostles, believers, teachers & evangelists,

- Touches people individually in conferences/multitude,

- Speaks through her with power and authority,

- Takes people into gift of laughter when she preaches,

- Addresses situations the body of Christ is facing,

- Unites the people in the region,

- Confirms His word through her with each prayer & message shared,

- Speaks through her so people hear His words in their own language, especially when the translators also experience the gift of laughter and stop translating,

- Directs her path to speak life into each situation whether God sends people to her to be re-encouraged or he asks her to pray with a pastor, the church, or someone in a store or a restaurant, etc.

Vision and word *For The Sake Of America* were given to internationally recognized prophets. They were not able to be 'boots on ground' in Georgia so they shared the facts with people they trusted.

Then, the vision and word were released to Sheila because she agreed to remain and fulfill upon the assignment after she traveled across country to Georgia for three weeks in October 2013.

She was not aware of the LORD's plan to extend her time to three years or that He would reveal such deep truth *For the Sake of America!*

However, the LORD confirmed in a specific vision that He sent her to Georgia because she asked for the assignment.

Since Georgia was not part of her conversations with the LORD she was a bit surprised until the LORD reminded her of her own words each time she witnessed the flow of the body of Christ in other nations He sent her to around the world. She hoped the LORD would send someone to bring the truth to the body of Christ in America.

When the LORD reminded her of her heart's desire, she realized in that moment He sent her to Georgia to be available during this critical time in our nation for His purpose, plan and promise to be made known to the people.

The LORD promised the prophets and Sheila if His people will stand in faith, humble themselves, repent for what He reveals to the body of Christ from Macon, Georgia to Moravian Falls, North Carolina then His truth will restore the people across America like a mighty flood.

God has taken Sheila around the world, church to church, business to business, nation to nation, set her before governors and kings without an extra coin or tunic.

Many confirm she walks in the five-fold ministry. She does not use a title because God does the work while He sends her as an apostle and prophet, and He orchestrates all arrangements for her to preach, teach, and evangelize.

People attending the conferences often say her segments are like watching someone walk out of the bible, share for a while and then, go right back in the bible, aka continue upon her journey in HIStory.

Made in the USA
Coppell, TX
02 February 2021

49412795R00164